MathFlare

Name: ____________________

Class: __________

Teacher: ____________________

Introduction

As parents and educators, we recognize the pivotal role mathematics plays in shaping a child's academic journey and future success. Yet, the path to mathematical proficiency can often seem daunting, fraught with challenges and complexities. That's where the transformative power of MathFlare Workbooks shine through, illuminating the way forward with clarity, precision, and purpose.

Introducing MathFlare Workbooks – a beacon of guidance, a testament to excellence, and a catalyst for achievement. Crafted with meticulous care and expertise, MathFlare Workbooks stand as paragons of educational excellence, designed to nurture young minds, ignite a passion for learning, and develop a deep-rooted understanding of mathematical concepts.

Picture this: your child eagerly delves into the pages of Mathflare Workbook, greeted by a step-by-step guide illuminated with vivid examples that demystify complex mathematical concepts. With each turn of the page, they embark on a journey of discovery, encountering thoughtfully curated practice questions that reinforce learning and hone problem-solving skills. And when they unveil the answers to those very questions, a sense of accomplishment blossoms within them – a tangible reward for their hard work and dedication.

But MathFlare Workbooks are more than just tools for learning; they are pathways to comprehension, fostering a deep-seated understanding of mathematical concepts through a sequential, logical flow. From fundamental principles to advanced problem-solving strategies, every chapter builds upon the last, ensuring a robust foundation upon which future knowledge can be constructed.

As parents, we yearn for nothing more than to see our children thrive, to witness the spark of inspiration ignited within them as they conquer academic challenges with confidence and poise. MathFlare Workbooks serve as partners in this noble endeavor, offering not just practice questions, but the keys to unlocking a world of opportunity.

And for teachers, MathFlare Workbooks stand as invaluable allies in the quest to cultivate mathematical proficiency in the classroom. With answers readily available, instructors can focus on guiding and nurturing their students, confident in the knowledge that MathFlare Workbooks provide a solid framework upon which to build.

In the pages of MathFlare Workbooks, we find not just the promise of academic excellence, but the seeds of a brighter tomorrow. So let us embrace the power of mathematics, let us champion the journey of learning, and let us pave the way for a generation of young minds poised to shape the world. With MathFlare Workbooks as our guide, the possibilities are infinite, and the future, bright.

Table of Contents

MathFlare
Grade 5
MATH WORKBOOK
Step by Step Guide and Essential Practice with Answers
Multiplication Division
Place Value and Expanded Notations
Fractions and Geometry
Unit Conversion
MathFlare Publishing

MathFlare
Grade 5-6
MATH WORKBOOK
Step by Step Guide and Essential Practice with Answers
Multiplication Division
Place Value and Expanded Notations
Fractions and Geometry
Units and Statistics
MathFlare Publishing

MathFlare
Grade 6
MATH WORKBOOK
Step by Step Guide and Essential Practice with Answers
Integers and Statistics
Arithmetic and Pre-Algebra
Fractions and Geometry
Ratio and Percentage
MathFlare Publishing

MathFlare
Grade 6-7
MATH WORKBOOK
Step by Step Guide and Essential Practice with Answers
Arithmetic and Pre-Algebra
Ratio, Percent Proportion
Geometry
Statistics
MathFlare Publishing

MathFlare
Grade 7
MATH WORKBOOK
Step by Step Guide and Essential Practice with Answers
Pre-Algebra
Ratio, Percent Proportion
Geometry
Statistics
MathFlare Publishing

MathFlare
Grade 7-8
MATH WORKBOOK
Step by Step Guide and Essential Practice with Answers
Pre-Algebra
Ratio, Percent Proportion
Geometry and Cartesian Plane
Statistics
MathFlare Publishing

MathFlare
Grade 8-9
MATH WORKBOOK
Step by Step Guide and Essential Practice with Answers
Pre-Algebra
Ratio, Proportion and Percentage
Linear Equations
Geometry and Cartesian Plane
MathFlare Publishing

MathFlare
Grade 8
MATH WORKBOOK
Step by Step Guide and Essential Practice with Answers
Pre-Algebra
Percentage
Linear Equations
Geometry
MathFlare Publishing

Addition and Subtraction

Addition

Adding is like putting things together to see how many we have altogether.

For instance, imagine we have 2 colorful blocks. Then, we add 3 more blocks. How many blocks do we have in total?

Let's count them together. 1, 2, 3, 4, 5.

Exactly! We have 5 blocks altogether! We show this with a plus sign (+) like this:

$$2 + 3 = 5.$$

Let's try another one.

If we have 5 pencils and we add four more pencils, how many pencils do we have in total?

Right, we have 9 pencils! We can write it down like this:

$$5 + 4 = 9.$$

Adding is fun! It helps us figure out how many things we have when we put them all together.

Let's solve a problem from the exercises.

$$\begin{array}{r} 11 \\ +\ 3 \\ \hline 14 \end{array}$$

Subtraction

Subtraction is all about taking things away or finding out how much is left.

Imagine you have a basket of 5 apples. Now, let's pretend you ate 2 of those yummy apples. How many do you have left?

Let's count them together. 1, 2, 3. Yes, you got it! You have 3 apples left!

We use this special sign "-" to show that we're taking away some apples.

Now, let's try another one! Imagine you have a bag full of 8 colorful marbles. Now, let's say you give away 3 of them to your friend. How many marbles are still in your bag?

Let's count them together. 1, 2, 3, 4, 5. Yes, you're correct! You have 5 marbles left!

We can write it down like this: 8 - 3 = 5.

Subtraction helps us figure out what's left after we take some away.

Let's solve a problem from the exercises.

$$
\begin{array}{r}
14 \\
-\ 10 \\
\hline
4 \\
\hline
\end{array}
$$

Commutative Property of Addition

The commutative property of addition tells us that it doesn't matter which order we add numbers together; we'll still get the same answer.

For instance: Imagine you have some colorful blocks.

Let's say you have 3 blue blocks and 2 red blocks.

Now, if we add them together, we get 5 blocks total, right? 3 (blue) + 2 (red) = 5.

But guess what? We can also add them in a different order!

Let's try adding the red blocks first, then the blue ones.

So, we have 2 (red) + 3 (blue).

Let's count them together. 1, 2, 3, 4, 5!

Yes, we still get 5 blocks in total!

It doesn't matter if we add the blue blocks first or the red ones first, we still end up with the same number of blocks.

Let's solve a problem from the exercises.

$$2 + \underline{9} = 9 + 2$$

$$\text{or} \quad 11 = 11$$

$$\underline{3} + 8 = 8 + 3$$

$$\text{or} \quad 11 = 11$$

<u>Addition and Subtraction Activities</u>

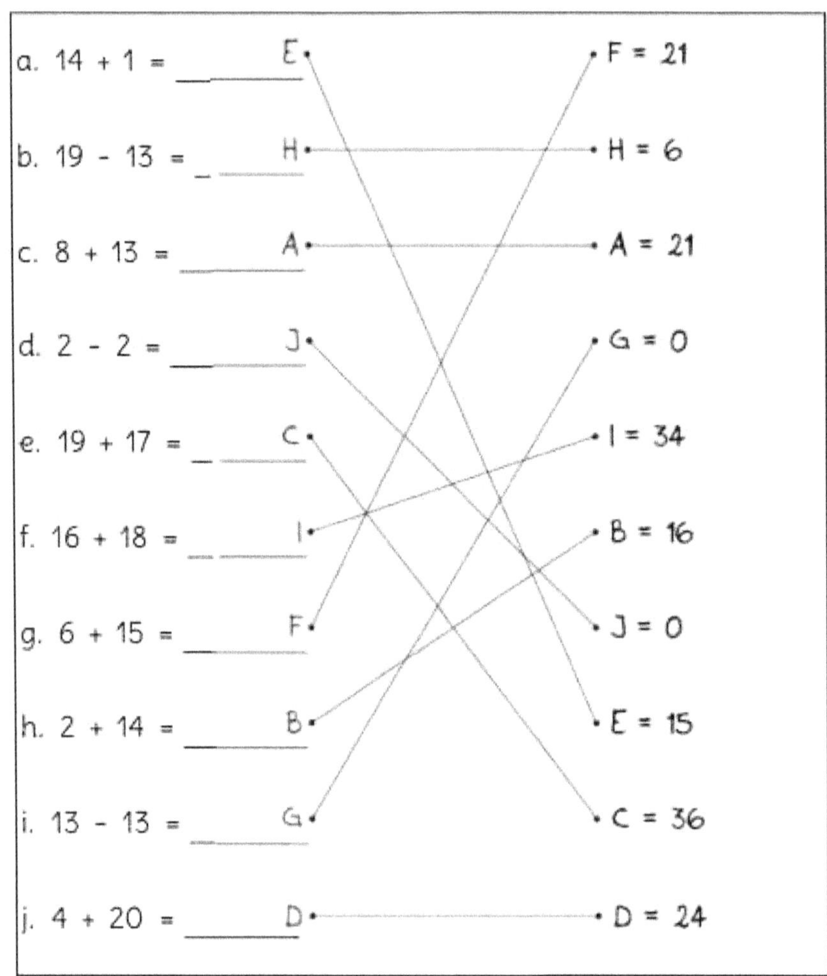

<u>Word Problems</u>

Word problems are like little puzzles that help us use addition in real-life situations.

For instance:

1. Jake has 6 carrots. He gets 2 more carrots. How many carrots does he have now?

To find out how many carrots he has now, we add the number of carrots he started with (6) to the number of carrots he got (2).

MathFlare -Addition and Subtraction 1st Grade

So, we add 6 + 2, which equals 8.

Jake now has 8 carrots in total!

Let's solve a problem:

Yesterday, Ray earned $1, and today, Ray earned $5. How much money did Ray earn in total?

$$
\begin{array}{rl}
1 & \text{Ray earned yesterday} \\
+\ 5 & \text{Ray earned today} \\
\hline
6 & \text{Ray earned \$6 in total}
\end{array}
$$

2. Jake saved up 4 dollars to buy pencils. He spent 2 dollars on it. How much money does he have left?

To solve this problem, we need to start with the number of dollars Jake started with and subtract the number of dollars he spent on the pencils.

So, we subtract 2 from 4, which equals 2:

Jake has 2 dollars left after buying the pencils.

Let's solve a problem:

Michele had 3 gloves. She lost 2 of them. How many gloves does Michele have left?

$$
\begin{array}{rl}
3 & \text{Michele had 3 gloves} \\
-\ 2 & \text{Michele lost 2 gloves} \\
\hline
1 & \text{Michele has 1 glove left}
\end{array}
$$

We need to understand what the problem is asking and what information it provides. Then, we can use addition or subtraction, depending on whether we're combining or taking away objects, to find the answer.

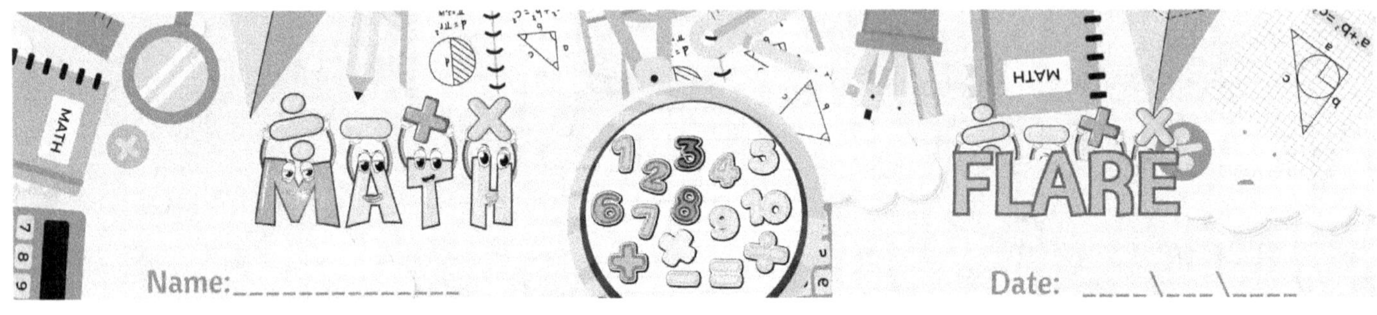

Addition: 1 through 20

Find the Sum.

1. 10
+ 14
____

2. 17
+ 2
____

3. 15
+ 1
____

4. 10
+ 18
____

5. 15
+ 12
____

6. 4
+ 9
____

7. 4
+ 7
____

8. 3
+ 10
____

9. 6
+ 17
____

10. 7
+ 14
____

11. 18
+ 17
____

12. 14
+ 15
____

13. 13
+ 16
____

14. 10
+ 7
____

15. 6
+ 11
____

16. 3
+ 19
____

17. 16
+ 16
____

18. 5
+ 2
____

19. 19
+ 17
____

20. 14
+ 1
____

Name:________________   Date: ____________

21. 1 + 7	22. 5 + 13	23. 9 + 12	24. 14 + 12	25. 4 + 3
26. 7 + 6	27. 2 + 13	28. 19 + 3	29. 9 + 19	30. 11 + 4
31. 13 + 5	32. 9 + 5	33. 12 + 8	34. 3 + 2	35. 11 + 9
36. 4 + 6	37. 14 + 11	38. 13 + 3	39. 8 + 2	40. 13 + 14
41. 2 + 17	42. 9 + 15	43. 11 + 17	44. 14 + 20	45. 5 + 5

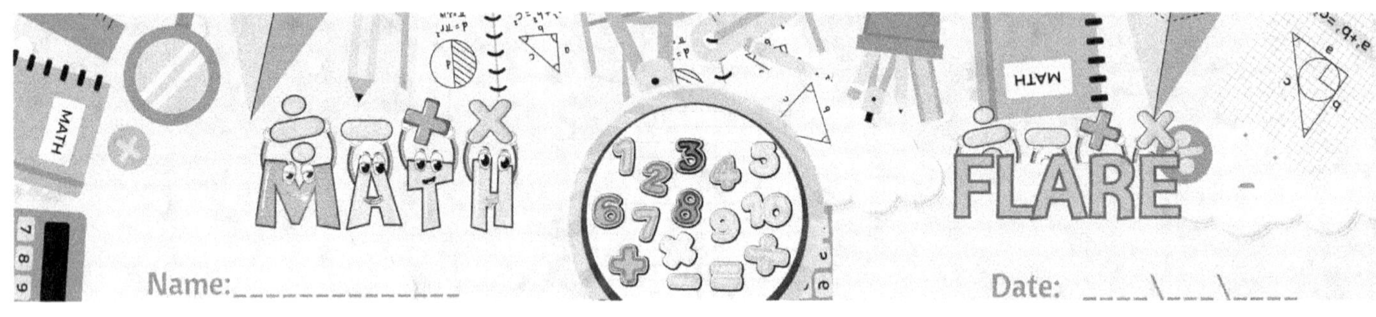

46. 1 + 15	47. 2 + 14	48. 19 + 1	49. 12 + 11	50. 20 + 18
51. 15 + 9	52. 7 + 7	53. 11 + 19	54. 17 + 8	55. 11 + 1
56. 1 + 14	57. 2 + 9	58. 17 + 14	59. 18 + 4	60. 1 + 17
61. 1 + 20	62. 3 + 13	63. 20 + 5	64. 12 + 4	65. 3 + 1
66. 8 + 15	67. 4 + 16	68. 13 + 20	69. 3 + 14	70. 13 + 8

Name:_______________   Date: ____________

71.	72.	73.	74.	75.
14 + 10	6 + 16	14 + 7	20 + 12	8 + 10

76.	77.	78.	79.	80.
7 + 11	7 + 4	6 + 18	2 + 10	12 + 2

81.	82.	83.	84.	85.
2 + 12	10 + 3	11 + 3	11 + 2	16 + 7

86.	87.	88.	89.	90.
8 + 7	1 + 13	11 + 6	4 + 11	13 + 19

91.	92.	93.	94.	95.
18 + 16	10 + 19	11 + 15	19 + 13	15 + 16

Name:_________________   Date: ______________

96. 16 + 13	97. 9 + 14	98. 7 + 12	99. 16 + 18	100. 14 + 19
101. 4 + 1	102. 4 + 14	103. 10 + 17	104. 18 + 14	105. 13 + 1
106. 9 + 3	107. 14 + 13	108. 13 + 11	109. 12 + 16	110. 3 + 4
111. 11 + 8	112. 4 + 15	113. 17 + 20	114. 10 + 6	115. 11 + 7
116. 6 + 19	117. 13 + 10	118. 16 + 17	119. 6 + 3	120. 15 + 2

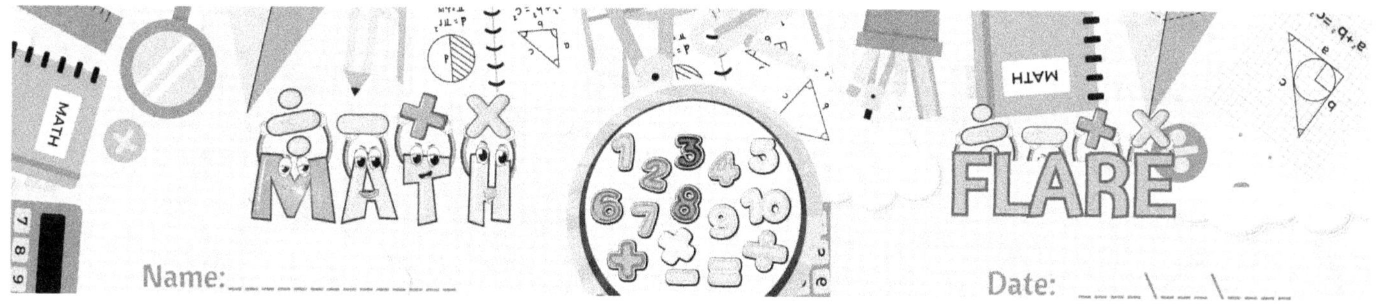

Addition: 1 through 20

Find the Sum.

121. $4 + 16 =$ _______________

122. $5 + 8 =$ _______________

123. $20 + 14 =$ _______________

124. $19 + 6 =$ _______________

125. $7 + 5 =$ _______________

126. $5 + 11 =$ _______________

127. $8 + 13 =$ _______________

128. $10 + 16 =$ _______________

129. $10 + 15 =$ _______________

130. $20 + 19 =$ _______________

131. $10 + 3 =$ _______________

132. $16 + 15 =$ _______________

133. $1 + 4 =$ _______________

134. $15 + 15 =$ _______________

135. $12 + 1 =$ _______________

136. $9 + 11 =$ _______________

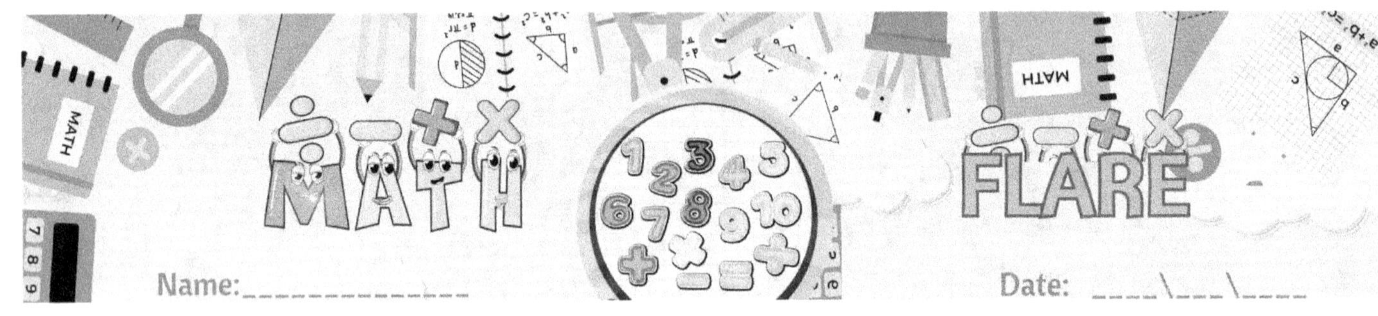

137. 8 + 15 = ________________

138. 4 + 17 = ________________

139. 16 + 4 = ________________

140. 2 + 5 = ________________

141. 19 + 7 = ________________

142. 2 + 15 = ________________

143. 11 + 20 = ________________

144. 19 + 20 = ________________

145. 8 + 10 = ________________

146. 3 + 16 = ________________

147. 17 + 16 = ________________

148. 6 + 3 = ________________

149. 11 + 5 = ________________

150. 14 + 16 = ________________

151. 11 + 12 = ________________

152. 13 + 5 = ________________

153. 6 + 16 = ________________

154. 13 + 13 = ________________

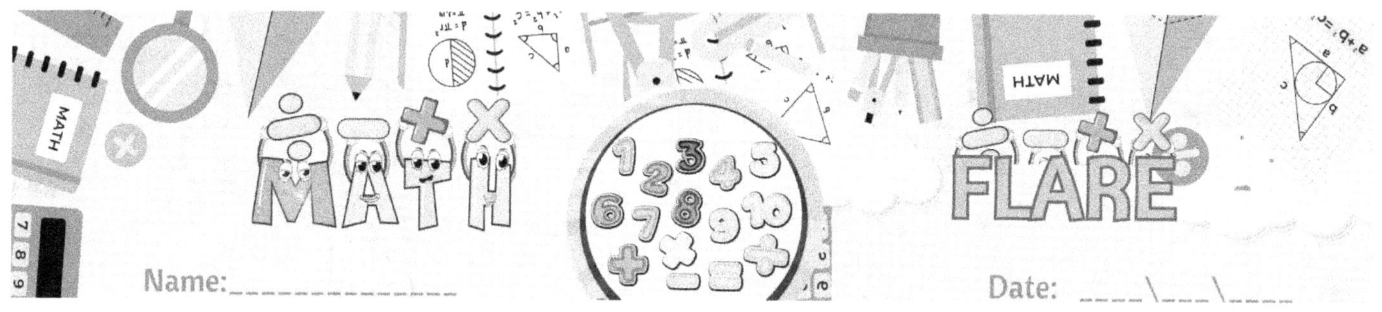

155. 20 + 17 = _______________

156. 18 + 1 = _______________

157. 9 + 4 = _______________

158. 2 + 3 = _______________

159. 5 + 1 = _______________

160. 5 + 15 = _______________

161. 8 + 2 = _______________

162. 19 + 12 = _______________

163. 14 + 12 = _______________

164. 9 + 2 = _______________

165. 7 + 11 = _______________

166. 10 + 5 = _______________

167. 14 + 7 = _______________

168. 14 + 17 = _______________

169. 12 + 14 = _______________

170. 15 + 5 = _______________

171. 7 + 15 = _______________

172. 11 + 6 = _______________

173. 18 + 17 = _______________

174. 8 + 3 = _______________

175. 3 + 10 = _______________

176. 1 + 14 = _______________

177. 12 + 15 = _______________

178. 6 + 12 = _______________

179. 6 + 11 = _______________

180. 4 + 14 = _______________

181. 7 + 13 = _______________

182. 8 + 9 = _______________

183. 8 + 14 = _______________

184. 7 + 3 = _______________

185. 11 + 4 = _______________

186. 10 + 11 = _______________

187. 6 + 20 = _______________

188. 9 + 13 = _______________

189. 5 + 7 = _______________

190. 19 + 17 = _______________

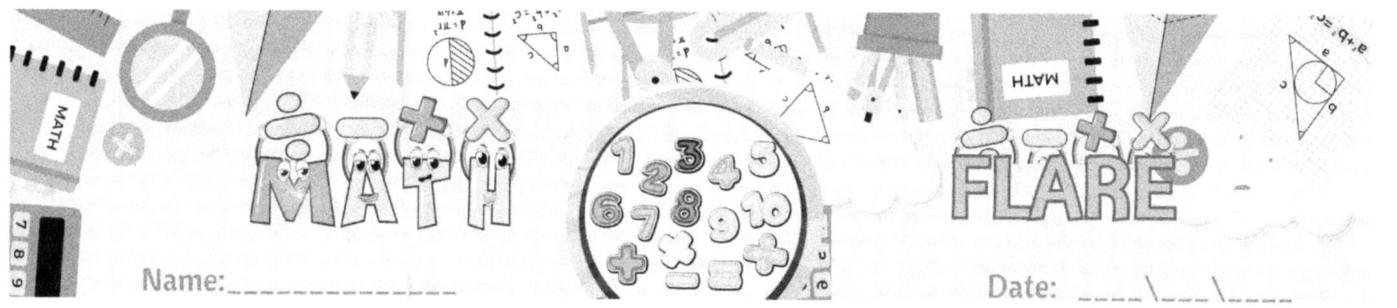

191. 11 + 16 = _______________

192. 13 + 19 = _______________

193. 3 + 3 = _______________

194. 12 + 2 = _______________

195. 11 + 2 = _______________

196. 18 + 14 = _______________

197. 18 + 5 = _______________

198. 13 + 18 = _______________

199. 19 + 11 = _______________

200. 9 + 12 = _______________

201. 1 + 12 = _______________

202. 17 + 7 = _______________

203. 10 + 20 = _______________

204. 14 + 10 = _______________

205. 18 + 12 = _______________

206. 2 + 8 = _______________

207. 20 + 9 = _______________

208. 12 + 9 = _______________

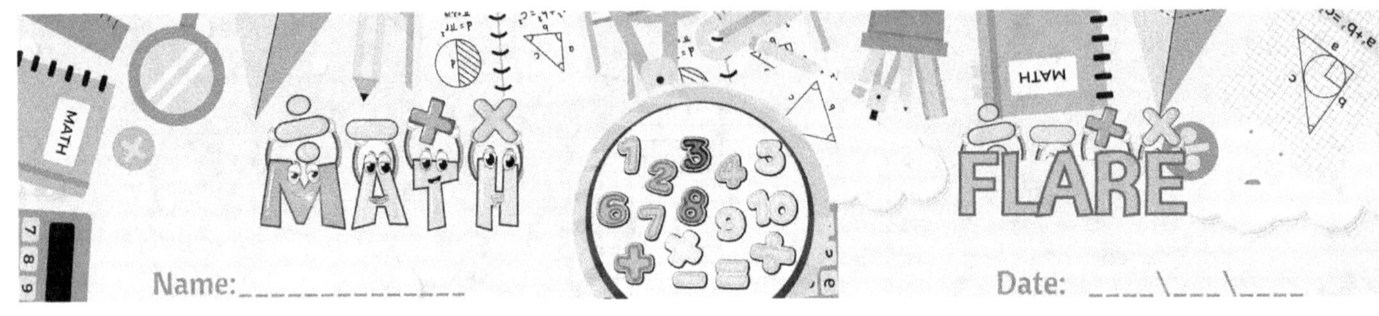

209. 20 + 5 = _______________

210. 3 + 14 = _______________

211. 6 + 10 = _______________

212. 16 + 10 = _______________

213. 7 + 18 = _______________

214. 15 + 2 = _______________

215. 18 + 2 = _______________

216. 12 + 10 = _______________

217. 3 + 20 = _______________

218. 5 + 5 = _______________

219. 12 + 18 = _______________

220. 1 + 18 = _______________

221. 4 + 7 = _______________

222. 5 + 4 = _______________

223. 10 + 13 = _______________

224. 8 + 11 = _______________

225. 16 + 8 = _______________

226. 2 + 12 = _______________

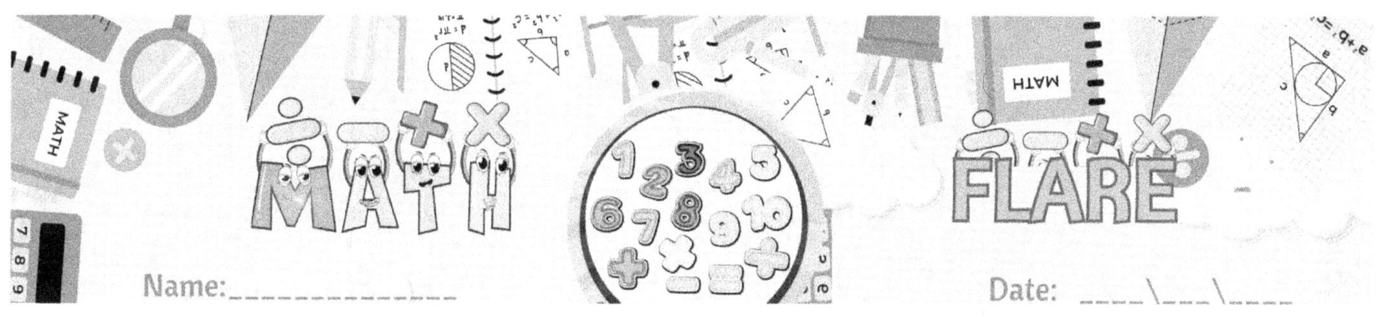

Name:________________   Date: _______________

227. 6 + 14 = ______________

228. 4 + 20 = ______________

229. 16 + 11 = ______________

230. 7 + 12 = ______________

231. 5 + 16 = ______________

232. 13 + 6 = ______________

233. 14 + 8 = ______________

234. 7 + 10 = ______________

235. 13 + 11 = ______________

236. 12 + 19 = ______________

237. 3 + 12 = ______________

238. 5 + 17 = ______________

239. 12 + 8 = ______________

240. 6 + 7 = ______________

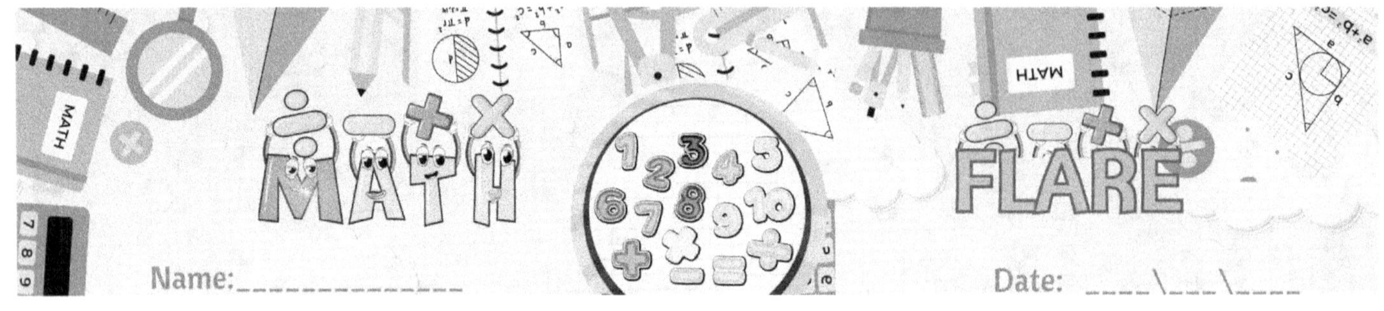

Subtraction: 1 through 20

Find the Difference.

241. $\begin{array}{r} 4 \\ -\ 2 \\ \hline \end{array}$	242. $\begin{array}{r} 9 \\ -\ 7 \\ \hline \end{array}$	243. $\begin{array}{r} 18 \\ -\ 14 \\ \hline \end{array}$	244. $\begin{array}{r} 6 \\ -\ 5 \\ \hline \end{array}$	245. $\begin{array}{r} 11 \\ -\ 3 \\ \hline \end{array}$
246. $\begin{array}{r} 20 \\ -\ 1 \\ \hline \end{array}$	247. $\begin{array}{r} 5 \\ -\ 2 \\ \hline \end{array}$	248. $\begin{array}{r} 3 \\ -\ 3 \\ \hline \end{array}$	249. $\begin{array}{r} 19 \\ -\ 15 \\ \hline \end{array}$	250. $\begin{array}{r} 20 \\ -\ 5 \\ \hline \end{array}$
251. $\begin{array}{r} 8 \\ -\ 8 \\ \hline \end{array}$	252. $\begin{array}{r} 9 \\ -\ 8 \\ \hline \end{array}$	253. $\begin{array}{r} 8 \\ -\ 4 \\ \hline \end{array}$	254. $\begin{array}{r} 13 \\ -\ 9 \\ \hline \end{array}$	255. $\begin{array}{r} 13 \\ -\ 5 \\ \hline \end{array}$
256. $\begin{array}{r} 2 \\ -\ 1 \\ \hline \end{array}$	257. $\begin{array}{r} 8 \\ -\ 1 \\ \hline \end{array}$	258. $\begin{array}{r} 15 \\ -\ 13 \\ \hline \end{array}$	259. $\begin{array}{r} 13 \\ -\ 12 \\ \hline \end{array}$	260. $\begin{array}{r} 19 \\ -\ 3 \\ \hline \end{array}$

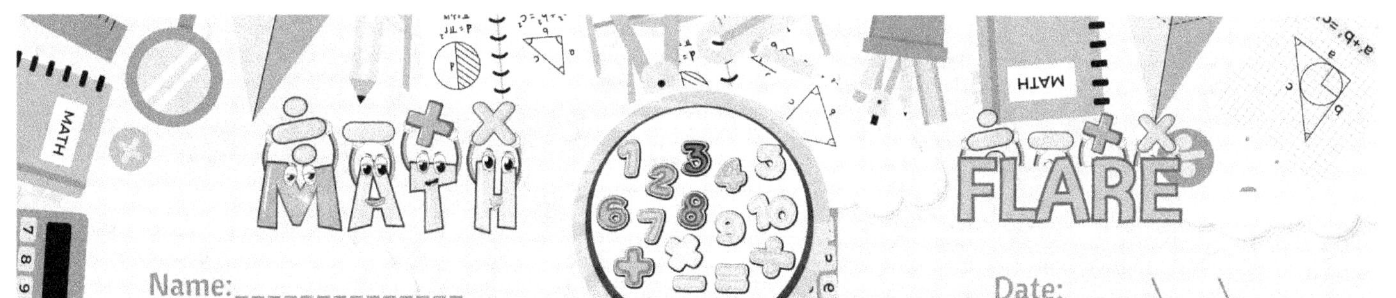

| 261. | 8
- 7 | 262. | 16
- 4 | 263. | 1
- 1 | 264. | 19
- 4 | 265. | 16
- 9 |

261. 8 − 7

262. 16 − 4

263. 1 − 1

264. 19 − 4

265. 16 − 9

266. 8 − 2

267. 12 − 8

268. 19 − 5

269. 19 − 1

270. 4 − 1

271. 3 − 2

272. 7 − 2

273. 18 − 6

274. 9 − 5

275. 12 − 5

276. 13 − 11

277. 18 − 1

278. 6 − 2

279. 12 − 3

280. 14 − 11

281. 15 − 5

282. 2 − 2

283. 14 − 5

284. 19 − 8

285. 17 − 12

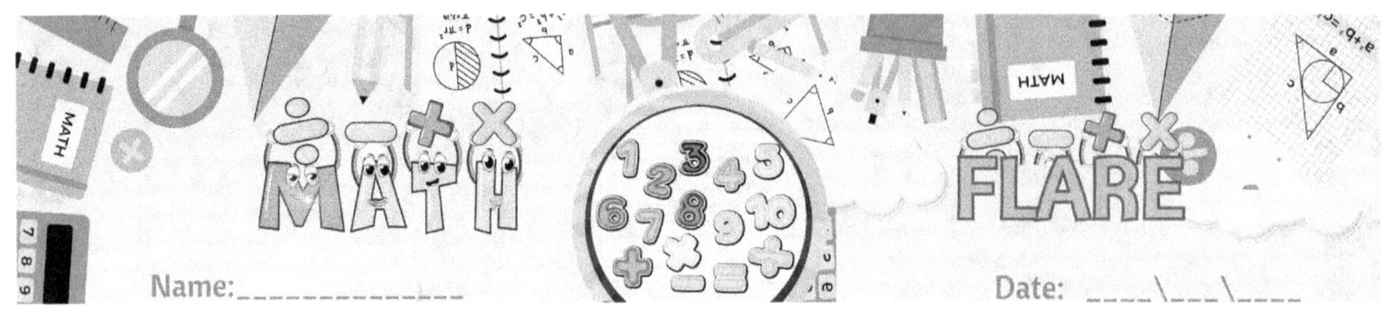

286. $\begin{array}{r} 13 \\ -\ 2 \\ \hline \end{array}$	287. $\begin{array}{r} 7 \\ -\ 5 \\ \hline \end{array}$	288. $\begin{array}{r} 15 \\ -\ 14 \\ \hline \end{array}$	289. $\begin{array}{r} 4 \\ -\ 3 \\ \hline \end{array}$	290. $\begin{array}{r} 16 \\ -\ 1 \\ \hline \end{array}$
291. $\begin{array}{r} 14 \\ -\ 9 \\ \hline \end{array}$	292. $\begin{array}{r} 10 \\ -\ 9 \\ \hline \end{array}$	293. $\begin{array}{r} 18 \\ -\ 10 \\ \hline \end{array}$	294. $\begin{array}{r} 8 \\ -\ 5 \\ \hline \end{array}$	295. $\begin{array}{r} 12 \\ -\ 10 \\ \hline \end{array}$
296. $\begin{array}{r} 8 \\ -\ 6 \\ \hline \end{array}$	297. $\begin{array}{r} 11 \\ -\ 5 \\ \hline \end{array}$	298. $\begin{array}{r} 16 \\ -\ 11 \\ \hline \end{array}$	299. $\begin{array}{r} 18 \\ -\ 18 \\ \hline \end{array}$	300. $\begin{array}{r} 10 \\ -\ 10 \\ \hline \end{array}$
301. $\begin{array}{r} 20 \\ -\ 4 \\ \hline \end{array}$	302. $\begin{array}{r} 20 \\ -\ 20 \\ \hline \end{array}$	303. $\begin{array}{r} 17 \\ -\ 1 \\ \hline \end{array}$	304. $\begin{array}{r} 10 \\ -\ 4 \\ \hline \end{array}$	305. $\begin{array}{r} 18 \\ -\ 8 \\ \hline \end{array}$
306. $\begin{array}{r} 6 \\ -\ 3 \\ \hline \end{array}$	307. $\begin{array}{r} 7 \\ -\ 4 \\ \hline \end{array}$	308. $\begin{array}{r} 14 \\ -\ 3 \\ \hline \end{array}$	309. $\begin{array}{r} 18 \\ -\ 9 \\ \hline \end{array}$	310. $\begin{array}{r} 9 \\ -\ 3 \\ \hline \end{array}$

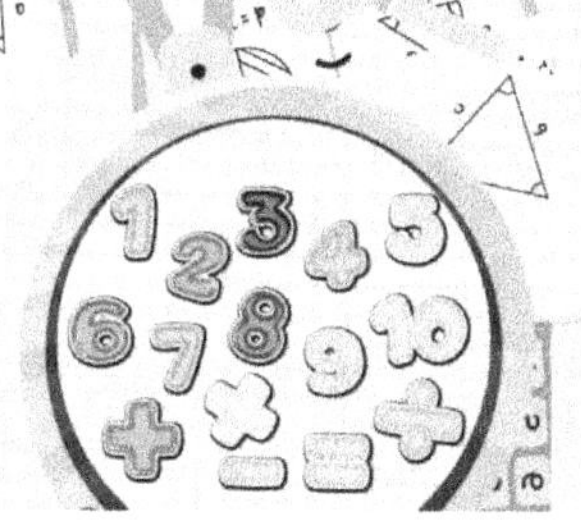
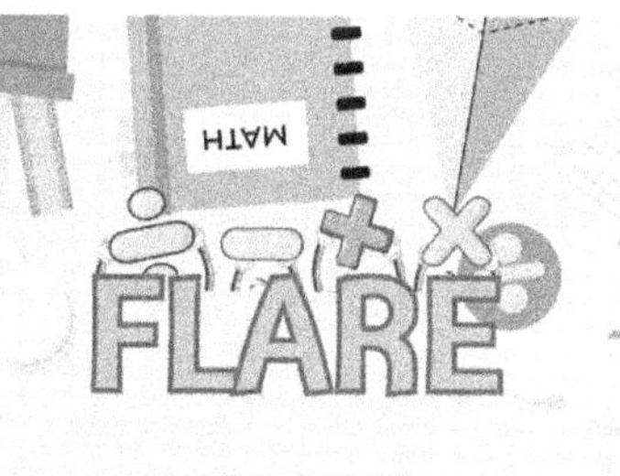

Name:________________   Date: ______________

311. 11 − 4	312. 17 − 14	313. 18 − 7	314. 12 − 2	315. 15 − 2
316. 5 − 1	317. 5 − 3	318. 14 − 13	319. 15 − 12	320. 20 − 12
321. 5 − 5	322. 18 − 17	323. 12 − 11	324. 13 − 10	325. 14 − 2
326. 18 − 13	327. 17 − 5	328. 13 − 7	329. 17 − 13	330. 20 − 14
331. 7 − 3	332. 16 − 8	333. 19 − 13	334. 14 − 6	335. 16 − 2

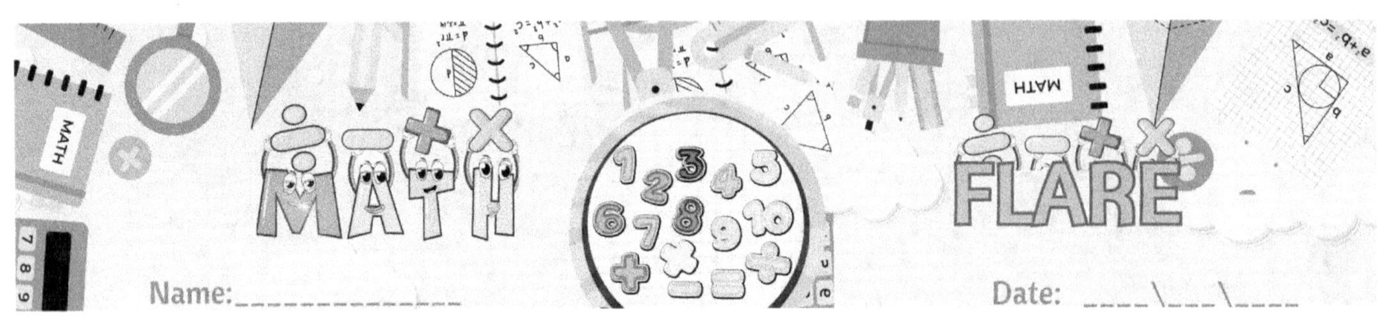

336. $\begin{array}{r} 10 \\ -\ 8 \\ \hline \end{array}$	337. $\begin{array}{r} 7 \\ -\ 6 \\ \hline \end{array}$	338. $\begin{array}{r} 15 \\ -\ 8 \\ \hline \end{array}$	339. $\begin{array}{r} 8 \\ -\ 3 \\ \hline \end{array}$	340. $\begin{array}{r} 15 \\ -\ 4 \\ \hline \end{array}$
341. $\begin{array}{r} 20 \\ -\ 13 \\ \hline \end{array}$	342. $\begin{array}{r} 10 \\ -\ 6 \\ \hline \end{array}$	343. $\begin{array}{r} 14 \\ -\ 10 \\ \hline \end{array}$	344. $\begin{array}{r} 20 \\ -\ 3 \\ \hline \end{array}$	345. $\begin{array}{r} 18 \\ -\ 2 \\ \hline \end{array}$
346. $\begin{array}{r} 5 \\ -\ 4 \\ \hline \end{array}$	347. $\begin{array}{r} 11 \\ -\ 6 \\ \hline \end{array}$	348. $\begin{array}{r} 16 \\ -\ 3 \\ \hline \end{array}$	349. $\begin{array}{r} 17 \\ -\ 8 \\ \hline \end{array}$	350. $\begin{array}{r} 11 \\ -\ 7 \\ \hline \end{array}$
351. $\begin{array}{r} 17 \\ -\ 2 \\ \hline \end{array}$	352. $\begin{array}{r} 20 \\ -\ 11 \\ \hline \end{array}$	353. $\begin{array}{r} 16 \\ -\ 5 \\ \hline \end{array}$	354. $\begin{array}{r} 19 \\ -\ 10 \\ \hline \end{array}$	355. $\begin{array}{r} 12 \\ -\ 6 \\ \hline \end{array}$
356. $\begin{array}{r} 9 \\ -\ 2 \\ \hline \end{array}$	357. $\begin{array}{r} 6 \\ -\ 6 \\ \hline \end{array}$	358. $\begin{array}{r} 11 \\ -\ 1 \\ \hline \end{array}$	359. $\begin{array}{r} 17 \\ -\ 3 \\ \hline \end{array}$	360. $\begin{array}{r} 12 \\ -\ 4 \\ \hline \end{array}$

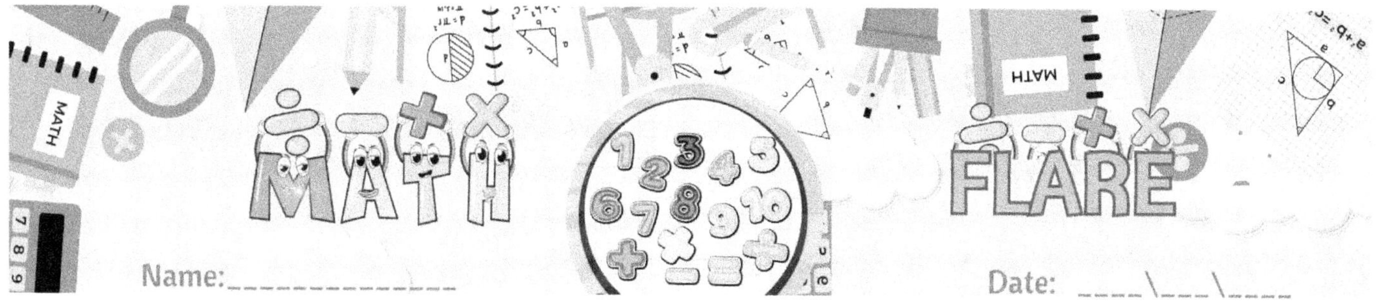

Name:______________________   Date: ______________

Subtraction: 1 through 20

Find the Difference.

361. 4 – 1 = ________________

362. 10 – 3 = ________________

363. 4 – 2 = ________________

364. 15 – 13 = ________________

365. 18 – 11 = ________________

366. 7 – 6 = ________________

367. 5 – 3 = ________________

368. 16 – 4 = ________________

369. 16 – 16 = ________________

370. 3 – 1 = ________________

371. 6 – 6 = ________________

372. 17 – 10 = ________________

373. 8 – 3 = ________________

374. 11 – 6 = ________________

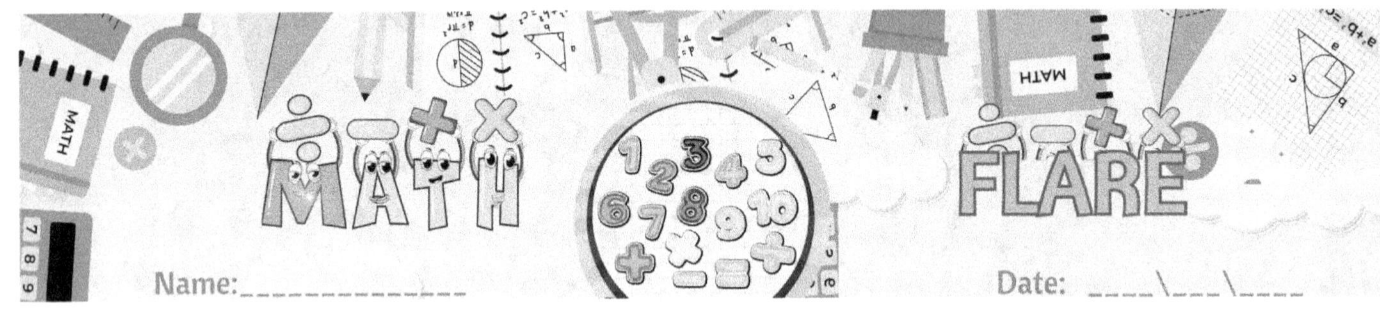

375. 7 - 4 = _______________

376. 3 - 2 = _______________

377. 1 - 1 = _______________

378. 13 - 9 = _______________

379. 11 - 10 = _______________

380. 2 - 2 = _______________

381. 14 - 4 = _______________

382. 20 - 17 = _______________

383. 6 - 4 = _______________

384. 7 - 3 = _______________

385. 12 - 6 = _______________

386. 2 - 1 = _______________

387. 17 - 15 = _______________

388. 15 - 7 = _______________

389. 6 - 5 = _______________

390. 16 - 10 = _______________

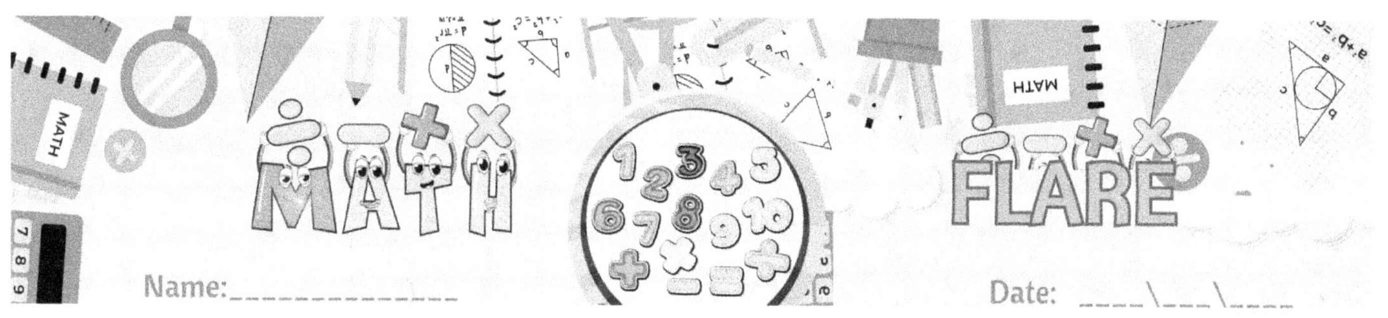

Name:_________________ Date: _____________

391. 12 - 2 = _______________   392. 18 - 16 = _______________

393. 17 - 4 = _______________   394. 20 - 19 = _______________

395. 5 - 5 = _______________   396. 18 - 12 = _______________

397. 12 - 10 = _______________   398. 17 - 11 = _______________

399. 5 - 4 = _______________   400. 13 - 11 = _______________

401. 9 - 4 = _______________   402. 19 - 8 = _______________

403. 9 - 3 = _______________   404. 13 - 2 = _______________

405. 10 - 5 = _______________   406. 5 - 2 = _______________

MathFlare -Addition and Subtraction 1st Grade

407. 19 - 4 = _______________

408. 20 - 16 = _______________

409. 20 - 8 = _______________

410. 15 - 4 = _______________

411. 9 - 2 = _______________

412. 18 - 1 = _______________

413. 20 - 10 = _______________

414. 10 - 8 = _______________

415. 4 - 3 = _______________

416. 11 - 4 = _______________

417. 18 - 5 = _______________

418. 9 - 5 = _______________

419. 11 - 3 = _______________

420. 18 - 2 = _______________

421. 19 - 14 = _______________

422. 13 - 5 = _______________

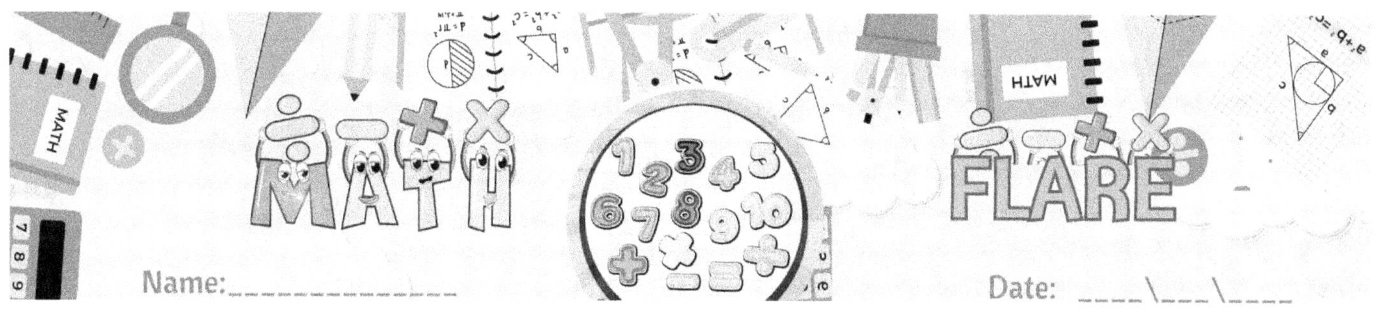

423. 8 - 4 = _______________

424. 20 - 12 = _______________

425. 6 - 2 = _______________

426. 5 - 1 = _______________

427. 14 - 1 = _______________

428. 10 - 10 = _______________

429. 13 - 10 = _______________

430. 3 - 3 = _______________

431. 10 - 9 = _______________

432. 18 - 8 = _______________

433. 18 - 14 = _______________

434. 17 - 7 = _______________

435. 9 - 1 = _______________

436. 14 - 11 = _______________

437. 8 - 7 = _______________

438. 12 - 11 = _______________

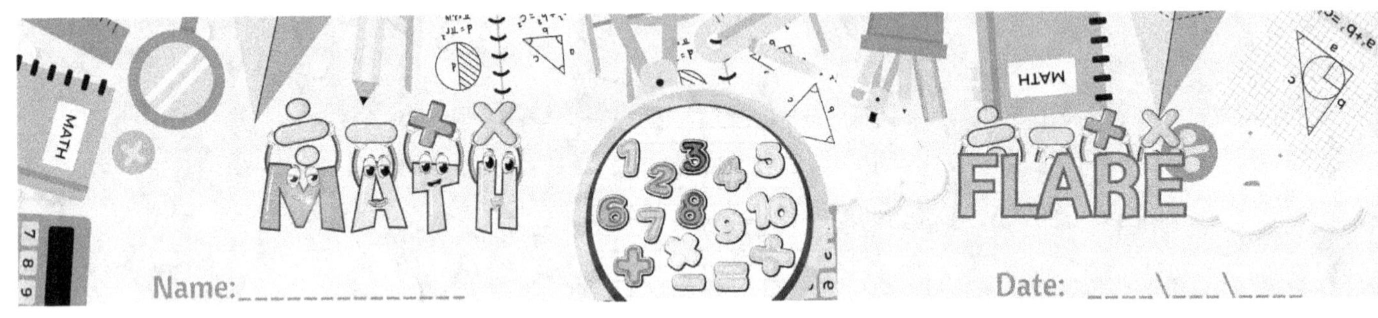

439. 16 - 14 = ___________

440. 19 - 11 = ___________

441. 17 - 6 = ___________

442. 13 - 8 = ___________

443. 19 - 13 = ___________

444. 9 - 7 = ___________

445. 16 - 12 = ___________

446. 11 - 1 = ___________

447. 19 - 6 = ___________

448. 16 - 2 = ___________

449. 17 - 14 = ___________

450. 13 - 13 = ___________

451. 19 - 3 = ___________

452. 12 - 8 = ___________

453. 15 - 14 = ___________

454. 8 - 5 = ___________

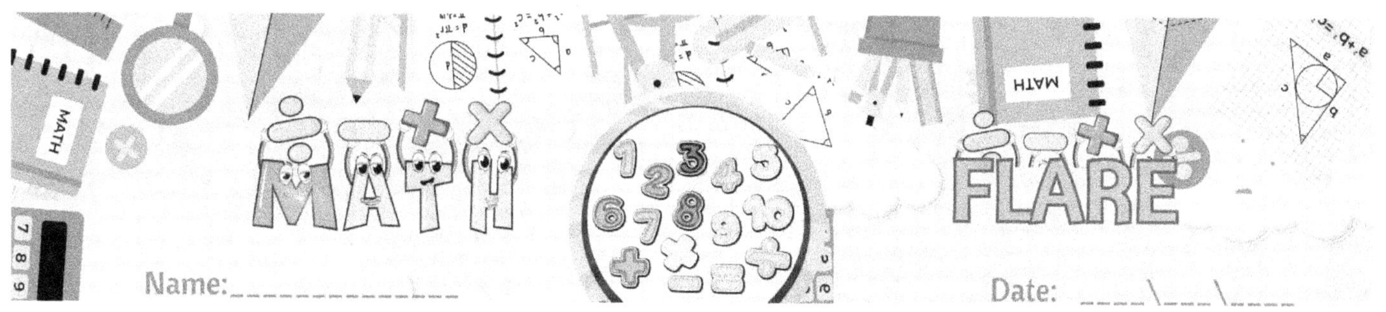

Name:_________________   Date: ____________

455. 10 - 7 = _______________

456. 15 - 3 = _______________

457. 20 - 4 = _______________

458. 14 - 5 = _______________

459. 6 - 1 = _______________

460. 8 - 2 = _______________

461. 18 - 4 = _______________

462. 12 - 4 = _______________

463. 7 - 2 = _______________

464. 8 - 8 = _______________

465. 17 - 2 = _______________

466. 13 - 1 = _______________

467. 18 - 13 = _______________

468. 4 - 4 = _______________

469. 8 - 1 = _______________

470. 12 - 5 = _______________

471. 11 - 5 = _______________

472. 14 - 6 = _______________

473. 19 - 1 = _______________

474. 17 - 5 = _______________

475. 19 - 7 = _______________

476. 14 - 3 = _______________

477. 16 - 8 = _______________

478. 12 - 7 = _______________

479. 8 - 6 = _______________

480. 20 - 6 = _______________

481. 17 - 13 = _______________

482. 14 - 10 = _______________

483. 13 - 3 = _______________

484. 20 - 13 = _______________

485. 18 - 15 = _______________

486. 13 - 4 = _______________

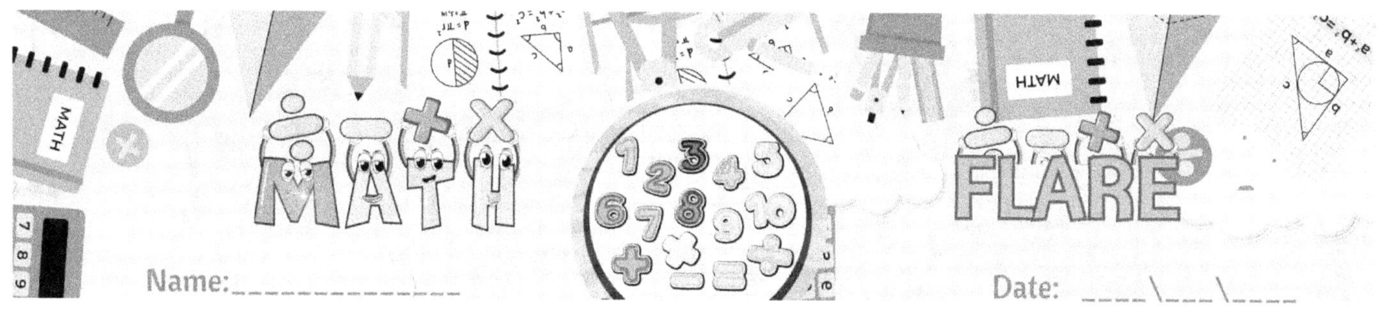

487. 14 - 2 = _______________

488. 7 - 5 = _______________

489. 18 - 18 = _______________

490. 15 - 1 = _______________

491. 9 - 6 = _______________

492. 18 - 17 = _______________

493. 19 - 2 = _______________

494. 15 - 15 = _______________

495. 11 - 8 = _______________

496. 11 - 2 = _______________

497. 12 - 9 = _______________

498. 19 - 15 = _______________

499. 16 - 7 = _______________

500. 14 - 9 = _______________

501. 13 - 6 = _______________

502. 15 - 11 = _______________

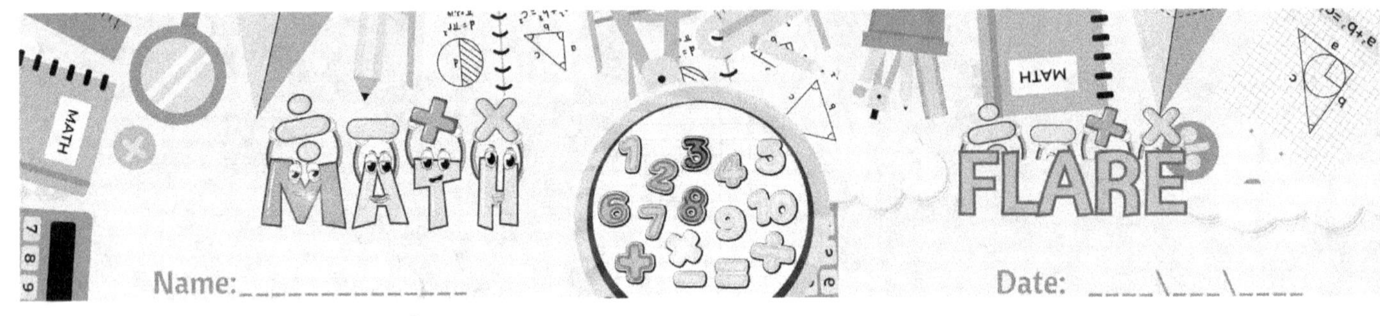

Commutative Property

Use the commutative property to fill the missing values.

503. 6 + __ = 7 + 6

504. __ + 2 = 2 + 5

505. 6 + 2 = __ + 6

506. __ + 2 = 2 + 8

507. 3 + __ = 1 + 3

508. 4 + __ = 2 + 4

509. 10 + __ = 2 + 10

510. 4 + 8 = __ + 4

511. 3 + 8 = __ + 3

512. 7 + __ = 3 + 7

513. __ + 6 = 6 + 10

514. __ + 1 = 1 + 8

515. 3 + 2 = __ + 3

516. 8 + 7 = 7 + __

517. __ + 5 = 5 + 2

518. __ + 6 = 6 + 9

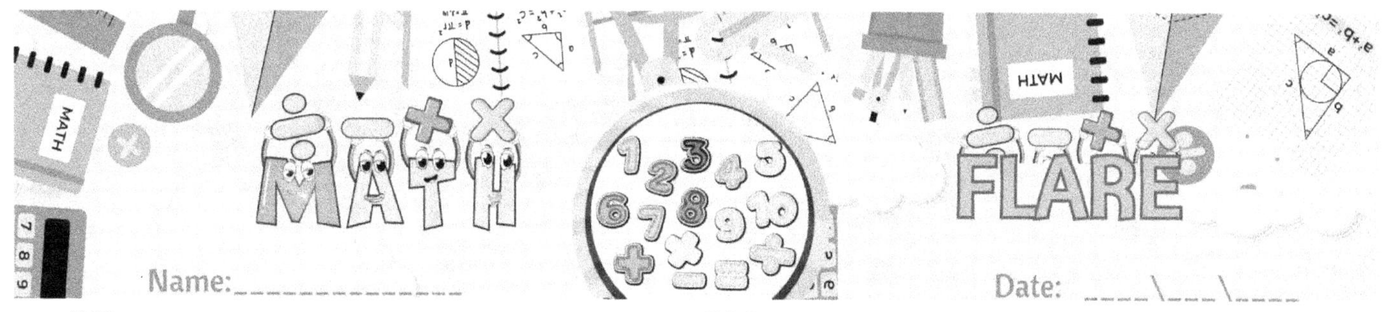

519. 8 + __ = 4 + 8

520. 6 + 8 = __ + 6

521. __ + 2 = 2 + 9

522. __ + 4 = 4 + 10

523. __ + 9 = 9 + 4

524. 2 + __ = 10 + 2

525. 5 + 7 = 7 + __

526. 4 + 7 = 7 + __

527. __ + 3 = 3 + 5

528. __ + 3 = 3 + 2

529. __ + 7 = 7 + 3

530. 2 + 6 = __ + 2

531. 7 + 10 = 10 + __

532. 6 + 9 = 9 + __

533. 6 + 3 = __ + 6

534. 7 + 1 = 1 + __

535. 2 + __ = 7 + 2

536. 5 + 1 = 1 + __

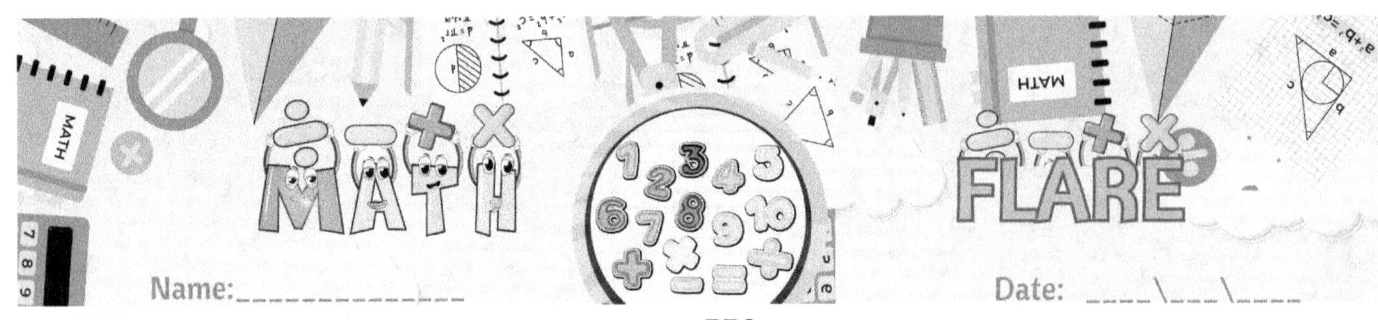

537. __ + 3 = 3 + 9

538. 3 + 5 = 5 + __

539. 4 + 5 = __ + 4

540. 9 + 4 = 4 + __

541. 2 + __ = 9 + 2

542. __ + 6 = 6 + 3

543. 1 + 5 = __ + 1

544. 5 + 9 = __ + 5

545. __ + 3 = 3 + 4

546. 1 + 9 = __ + 1

547. 6 + __ = 4 + 6

548. 8 + __ = 9 + 8

549. __ + 9 = 9 + 3

550. __ + 1 = 1 + 10

Name:________________   Date: _______________

Addition-Subtraction Activities

551.

a. 9 + 6 = _______ •	• D = 11
b. 1 - 1 = _______ •	• I = 3
c. 9 + 15 = _______ •	• H = 13
d. 17 + 19 = _______ •	• F = 0
e. 6 - 3 = _______ •	• J = 15
f. 18 - 2 = _______ •	• C = 16
g. 12 - 1 = _______ •	• E = 36
h. 10 + 3 = _______ •	• G = 17
i. 6 + 3 = _______ •	• A = 9
j. 14 + 3 = _______ •	• B = 24

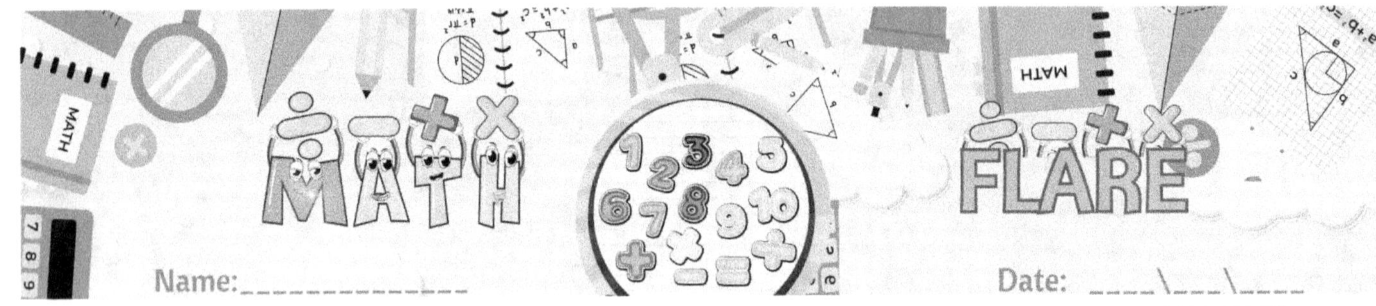

552.

a. 18 + 3 = _______ •   • E = 27

b. 9 + 15 = _______ •   • J = 32

c. 18 + 14 = _______ •   • B = 32

d. 9 + 18 = _______ •   • C = 24

e. 12 - 7 = _______ •   • G = 5

f. 17 - 3 = _______ •   • H = 7

g. 19 + 13 = _______ •   • D = 14

h. 18 + 6 = _______ •   • I = 21

i. 17 - 12 = _______ •   • F = 24

j. 12 - 5 = _______ •   • A = 5

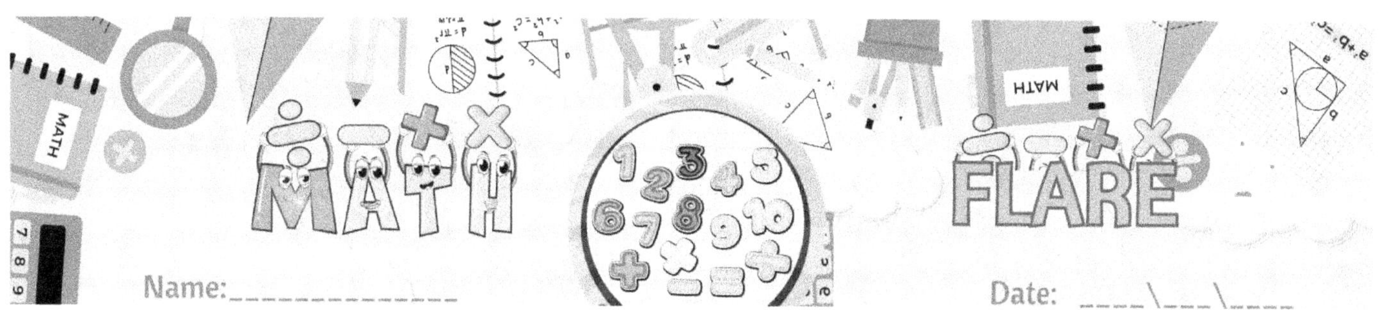

553.

a. 9 + 17 = _______ •	• D = 0
b. 20 − 6 = _______ •	• F = 2
c. 7 − 7 = _______ •	• I = 26
d. 3 + 12 = _______ •	• G = 14
e. 17 − 6 = _______ •	• E = 11
f. 1 + 14 = _______ •	• J = 15
g. 11 − 1 = _______ •	• A = 10
h. 17 − 1 = _______ •	• H = 0
i. 17 − 15 = _______ •	• C = 16
j. 2 − 2 = _______ •	• B = 15

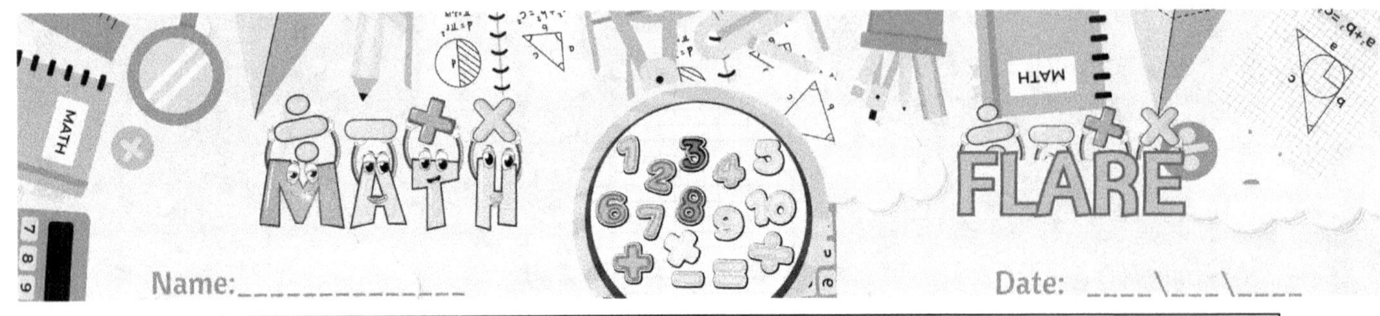

554.

a. 1 + 12 = _______ •	• E = 14
b. 10 + 8 = _______ •	• I = 0
c. 15 - 1 = _______ •	• C = 17
d. 20 - 17 = ______ •	• D = 13
e. 1 + 16 = _______ •	• A = 29
f. 4 - 4 = _______ •	• G = 3
g. 12 + 17 = ______ •	• H = 21
h. 4 + 11 = _______ •	• F = 7
i. 5 + 16 = _______ •	• B = 18
j. 18 - 11 = ______ •	• J = 15

Name:________________   Date: ____________

555.

a. 16 − 15 = _______ •	• C = 30
b. 11 + 6 = _______ •	• H = 28
c. 17 + 1 = _______ •	• G = 17
d. 18 + 4 = _______ •	• D = 22
e. 16 + 19 = _______ •	• B = 1
f. 19 + 17 = _______ •	• J = 14
g. 9 + 19 = _______ •	• F = 36
h. 16 + 20 = _______ •	• E = 36
i. 9 + 5 = _______ •	• I = 35
j. 14 + 16 = _______ •	• A = 18

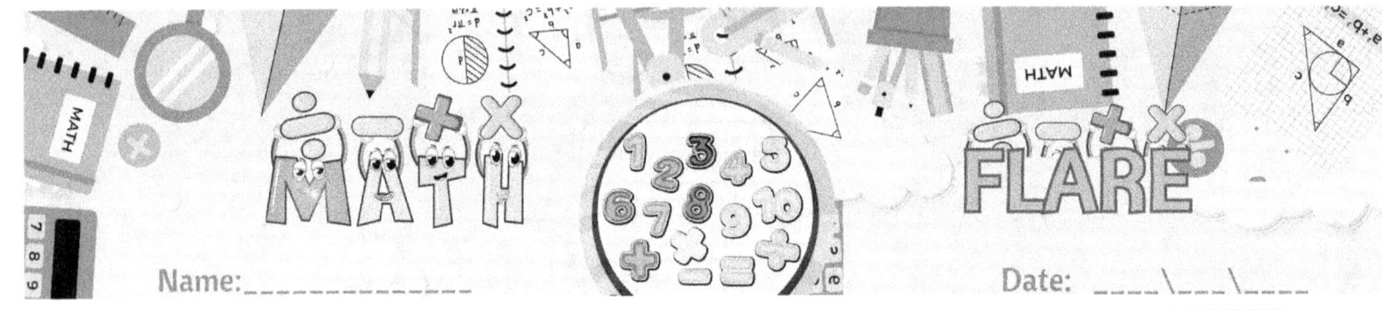

Name:_______________ Date: ___________

556.

a. 4 - 1 = _______ •	• J = 33
b. 15 - 5 = _______ •	• A = 0
c. 15 - 7 = _______ •	• I = 3
d. 18 + 15 = _______ •	• E = 8
e. 14 - 9 = _______ •	• C = 4
f. 18 - 6 = _______ •	• G = 5
g. 9 - 9 = _______ •	• B = 10
h. 9 - 1 = _______ •	• F = 8
i. 5 - 3 = _______ •	• D = 12
j. 1 + 3 = _______ •	• H = 2

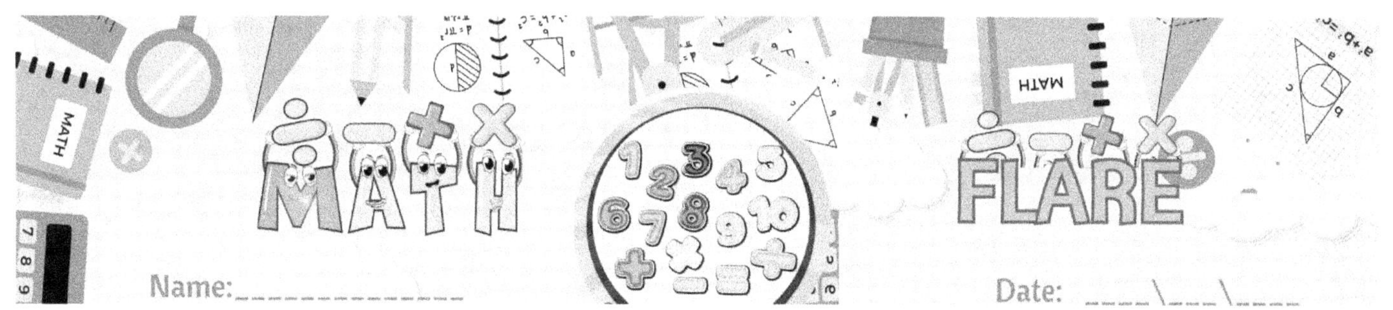

Name:_____________________   Date: _______________

557.

a. 12 + 14 = _______ •   • I = 4

b. 14 + 7 = _______ •   • G = 21

c. 4 - 4 = _______ •   • F = 2

d. 9 - 6 = _______ •   • H = 0

e. 16 - 16 = _______ •   • C = 3

f. 17 + 10 = _______ •   • D = 10

g. 15 - 11 = _______ •   • J = 26

h. 1 + 1 = _______ •   • E = 13

i. 11 + 2 = _______ •   • A = 27

j. 14 - 4 = _______ •   • B = 0

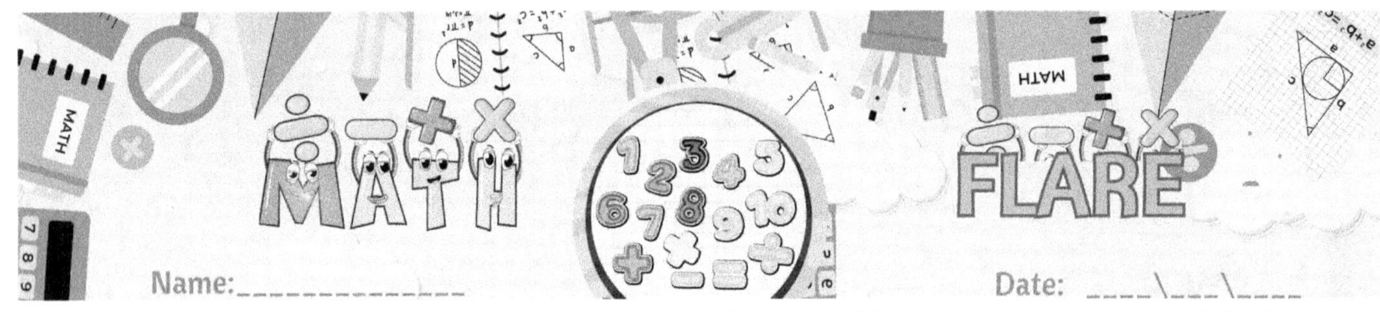

558.

a. 7 − 1 = _______ •	• J = 21
b. 20 + 2 = ______ •	• G = 11
c. 14 − 3 = ______ •	• B = 22
d. 1 + 15 = ______ •	• H = 16
e. 9 − 3 = ______ •	• D = 14
f. 13 + 8 = ______ •	• C = 6
g. 11 + 7 = ______ •	• I = 1
h. 15 − 14 = _____ •	• E = 6
i. 2 + 12 = ______ •	• A = 20
j. 4 + 16 = ______ •	• F = 18

Name:______________   Date: _______________

559.

a. 16 − 3 = _______ •	• I = 10
b. 10 + 15 = _______ •	• H = 29
c. 3 − 2 = _______ •	• F = 0
d. 9 − 9 = _______ •	• C = 0
e. 8 − 8 = _______ •	• A = 1
f. 5 − 5 = _______ •	• D = 8
g. 5 + 5 = _______ •	• G = 13
h. 9 − 1 = _______ •	• J = 32
i. 16 + 16 = _______ •	• B = 0
j. 18 + 11 = _______ •	• E = 25

560.

a. 20 − 3 = _______ •	• A = 9
b. 8 − 8 = _______ •	• G = 16
c. 13 − 7 = _______ •	• F = 28
d. 11 + 4 = _______ •	• J = 20
e. 11 + 9 = _______ •	• C = 27
f. 18 + 9 = _______ •	• I = 0
g. 17 − 8 = _______ •	• B = 15
h. 17 − 1 = _______ •	• E = 0
i. 16 + 12 = _______ •	• H = 6
j. 2 − 2 = _______ •	• D = 17

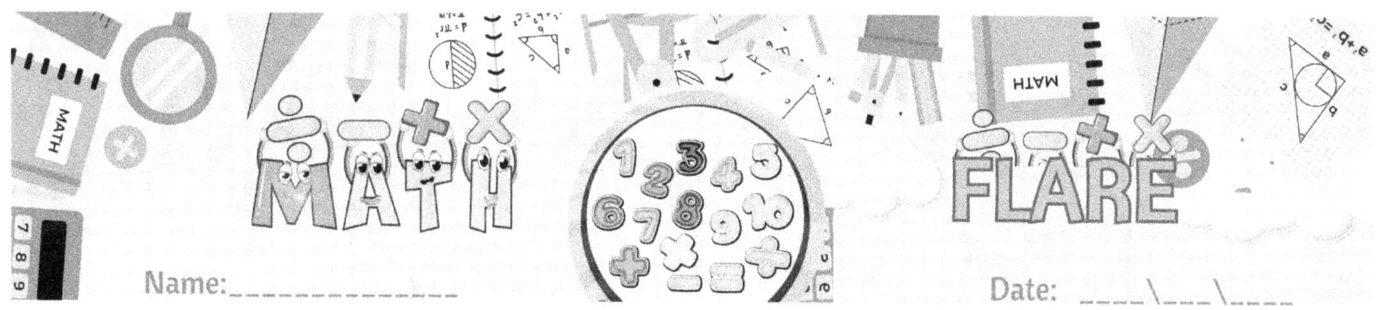

Addition Word Problems

561. Levi has 6 brushes. He gets 7 more brushes. How many brushes does he have now?

562. A pack of gum contains 2 pieces of gum. If 10 more pieces of gum are added to the pack, how many pieces of gum will the pack contain?

563. Jayden baked 3 cookies and 8 cupcakes. How many desserts did Jayden bake in total?

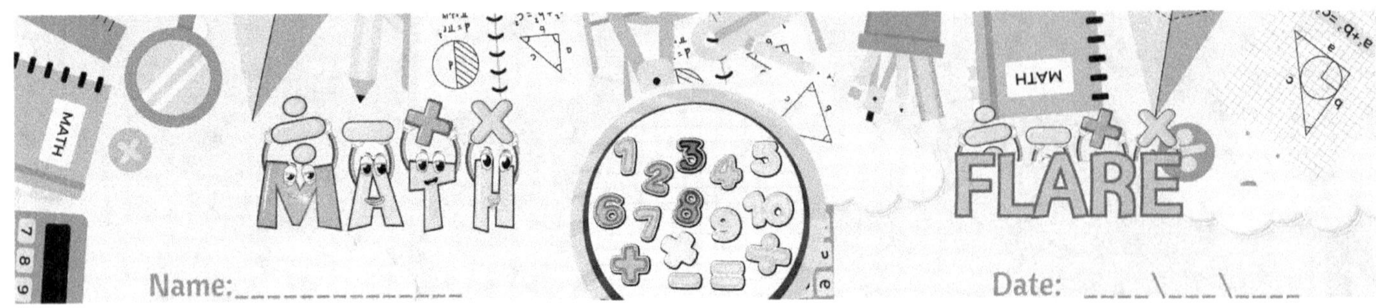

564. Christian has 8 rocks. He finds 9 more rocks. How many rocks does he have now?

565. At the beginning of the week, there were 5 folders in the bag. By the end of the week, 7 more folders were added to the bag. How many folders are in the bag now?

566. A soccer team scored 9 goals in the first half and 8 goals in the second half. What was the total score of the soccer team?

567. There are 9 calculators on the shelf. Lila puts 6 more calculators on the shelf. How many calculators are there on the shelf now?

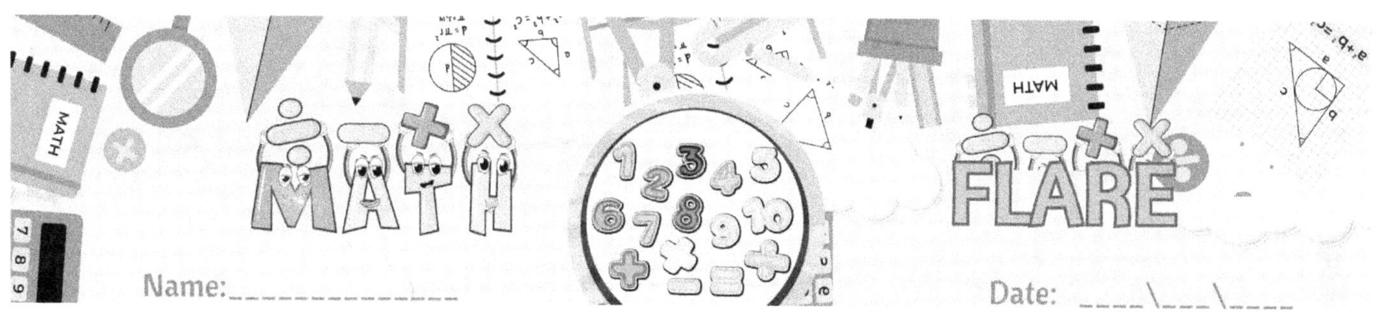

568. At the start of the school year, there were 8 students enrolled in English class. By the end of the year, 7 more students had enrolled. How many students were enrolled in English class at the end of the year?

569. At the store, Robert bought 4 globes. Later, Harper bought 7 globes from the same store. How many globes were bought in total?

570. Kaylee bought pizzas with 3 slices. Later, Kaylee bought some more pizzas with 5 slices. How many slices of pizzas does Kaylee have in total?

571. There are 9 parrots on a tree. 1 more parrots land on the tree. How many parrots are on the tree now?

572. Cameron had 7 dollars in the morning and earned 3 more dollars in the afternoon. How many dollars Cameron have in total?

573. Jace has 7 dollars and found 4 more dollars on the ground. How much money does Jace have now?

574. Miles has 9 red marbles and 3 blue marbles in a jar. How many marbles does Miles have in total?

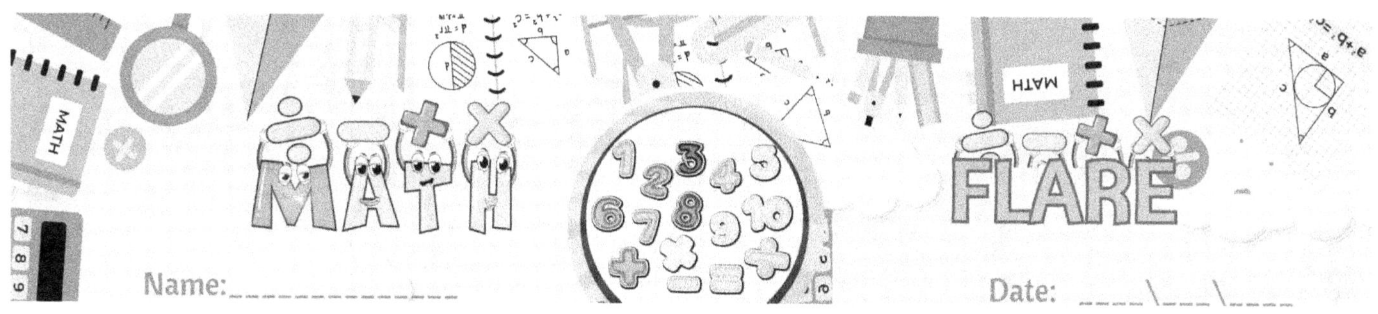

575. Nicholas has 9 apples and 3 oranges in a basket. How many fruits does Nicholas have in total?

576. Dominic has 6 pencils and 1 pens. If Dominic puts all the writing utensils in a case, how many writing utensils are in the case in total?

577. There were 3 people in line at the store. After 5 more people joined the line, how many people are in the line now?

578. A basket holds 7 watches. If 7 more watches are added to the basket, how many watches will the basket hold in total?

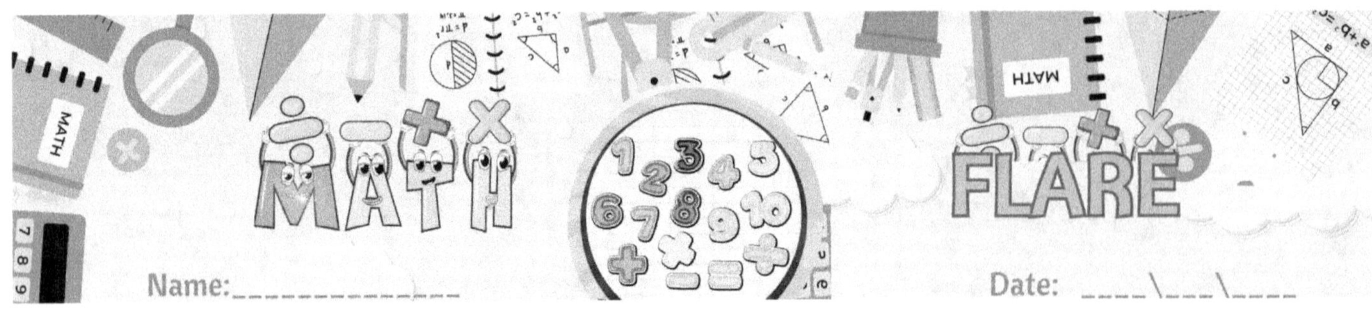

Name:___________________   Date: ___________

579. There are 5 violins in the bag. If 5 more violins are added, how many violins are in the bag now?

580. Everly has 9 syringes. She gets 2 more syringes. How many syringes does Everly have now?

581. Sadie planted 7 flowers in the morning and 9 flowers in the afternoon. How many flowers did Sadie plant?

582. Eva watched 5 movies last week and 8 movies this week. How many movies did Eva watch altogether?

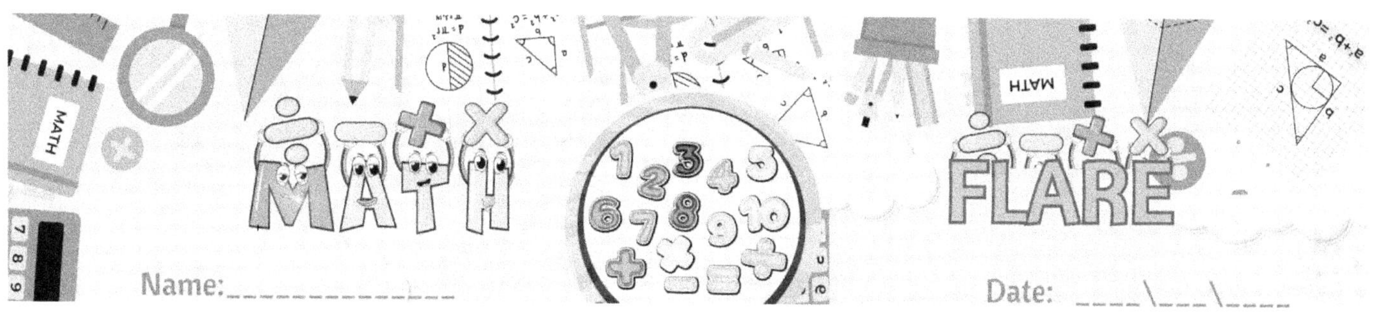

583. There are 10 kids playing on the playground. 1 more kids join them. How many kids are playing now?

584. James drove 2 miles in the morning and 6 miles in the evening. How many miles did James drive in total?

585. Roman had 10 dollars and earned 9 more dollars. How much money does Roman have now?

586. Bella has 3 breads. Her friend gives her 5 more breads. How many breads does Bella have now?

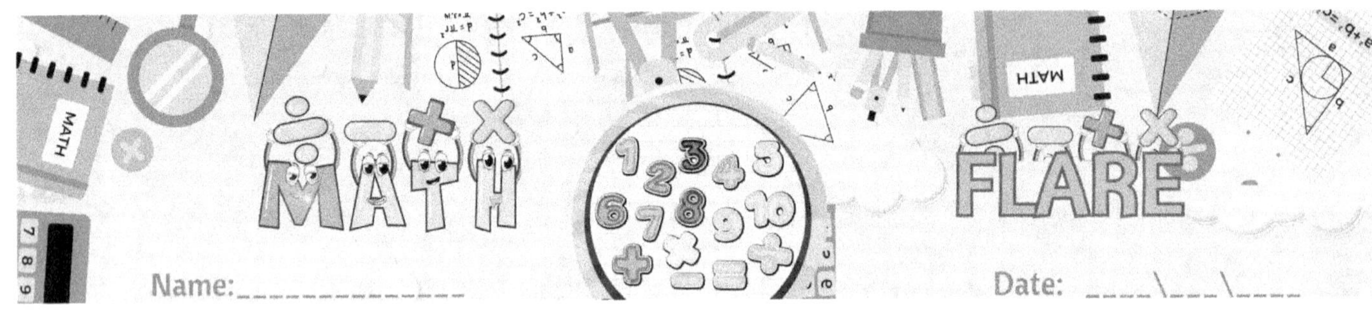

587. Emma wrote 10 pages of her book yesterday and 4 pages today. How many pages did she write in total?

588. Hunter made 2 cookies and Isabella made 5 cookies. How many cookies were made in total?

589. Maya walked 1 miles yesterday and 9 miles today. How many miles did Maya walk in total?

590. Kai has a basket with 3 radios in it. After buying 9 more radios, how many radios does Kai have in total?

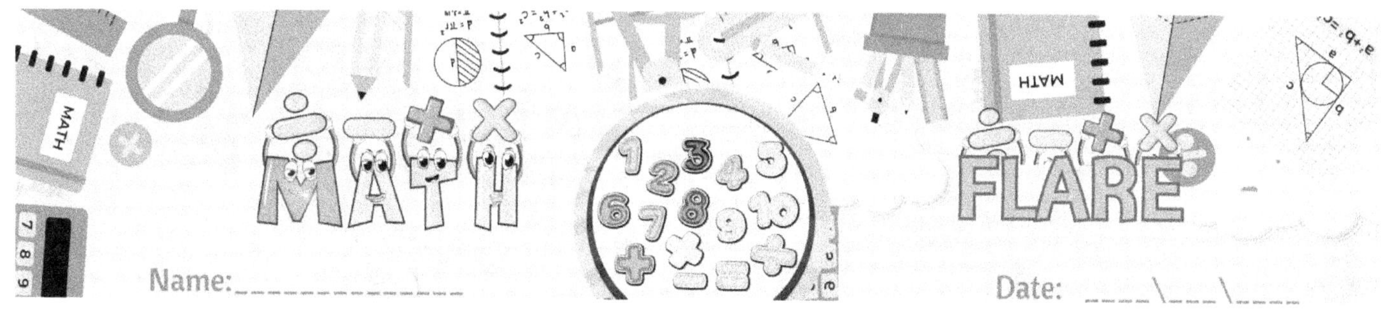

Subtraction Word Problems

591. A cake recipe requires 10 cups of sugar. Leah only has 1 cups of sugar. How many more cups of sugar does Leah need?

592. Charlotte has 2 soaps. She gave 2 soaps to Olivia. How many soaps does Charlotte have now?

593. Hazel wants to buy shoes, which costs 5 dollars. She has 5 dollars and plans to save the rest. How much more money does she need to save to buy shoes?

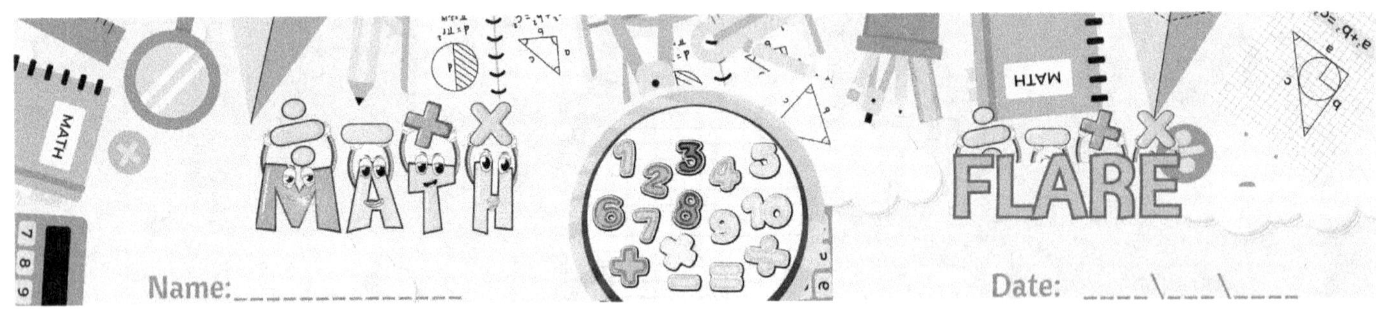

594. Molly baked a 2 cookies. 2 of them were chocolate chip cookies and the rest were oatmeal raisin cookies. How many oatmeal raisin cookies did Molly bake?

595. A recipe needs 9 cups of sugar. Elena added 8 cups of sugar. How many cups of sugar are still needed?

596. There were 1 students in a class. 1 of them were absent. How many students were present in the class?

597. There are 3 fish in a pond. Emily caught 1 fish. How many fish are left in the pond?

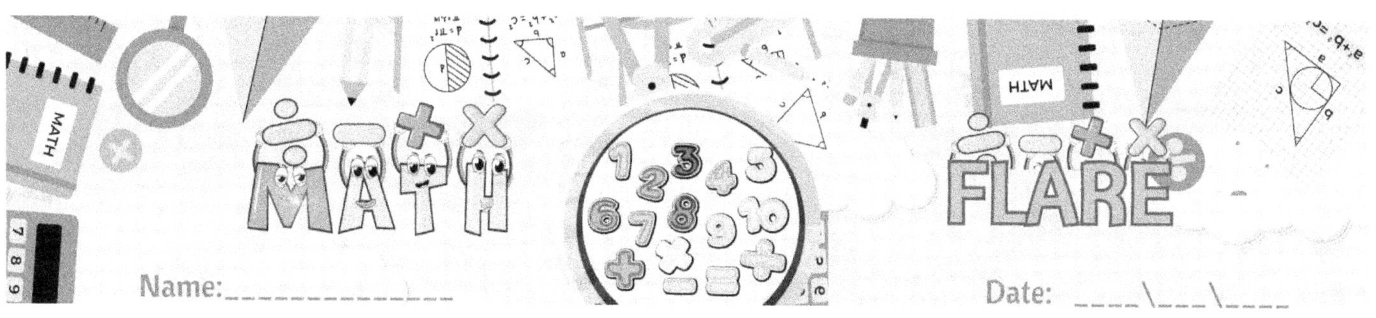

598. A box of pants weighs 4 pounds. If you remove 4 pounds from it, how much does it weigh now?

599. There is 1 dogs in a park. If 1 leave, how many dogs are left in the park?

600. A small bag of chips has 9 chips in it. Noah ate 2 chips. How many chips are left in the bag?

601. There are 7 pianos in a bag. Isabelle took 2 pianos out of the bag. How many pianos are still in the bag?

602. Genesis bought socks for 10 dollars. She later returned some socks and received a refund of 2 dollars. How much money did she end up spending on socks?

603. There are 9 fish in a tank. If 7 leave, how many fish are left in the tank?

604. Andrew saved up 2 dollars to buy rulers. He spent 2 dollars on it. How much money does he have left?

605. If you have 7 bananas and you give away 5, how many bananas do you have left?

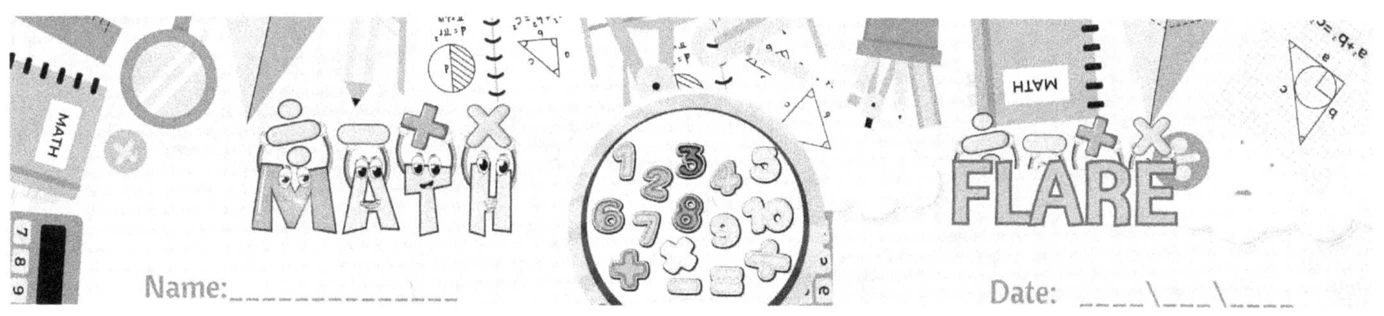

606. A pizza has 4 slices. Riley ate 4 slices. How many slices of pizza are left?

607. Anthony is 6 years old and Micah is 6 years old. What is the difference in their ages?

608. Christian had 2 dollars. He spent 2 dollars on a knives. How much money does Christian have left?

609. Gemma has 7 trees. She lost 2 of them. How many trees does Gemma have left?

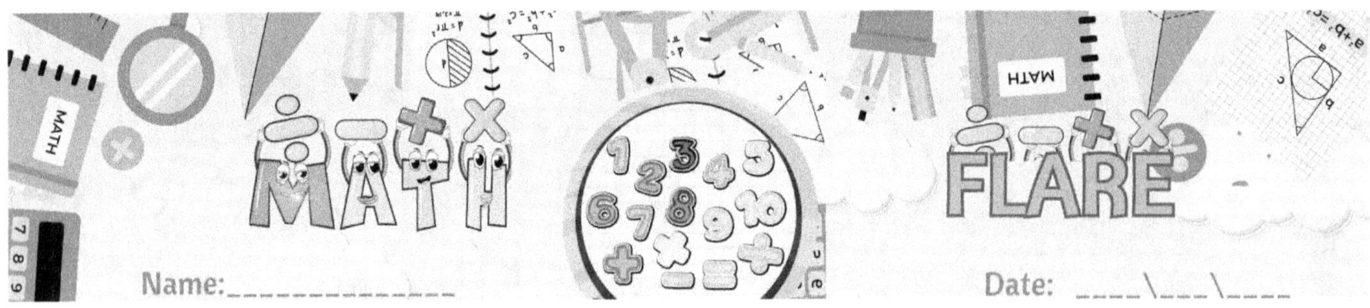

610. A box had 2 chocolates. Eva ate 2 chocolates. How many chocolates are left in the box?

611. Jordyn and Ellie went on a shopping spree and bought 8 clocks. After returning home, they realized that they didn't need 2 of them. How many clocks did they end up keeping?

612. Everleigh has 7 balls in her collection. She gave 5 of them to her friend. How many balls does Everleigh have now?

613. There are 7 turtles in a pond. If 7 leave, how many turtles are left in the pond?

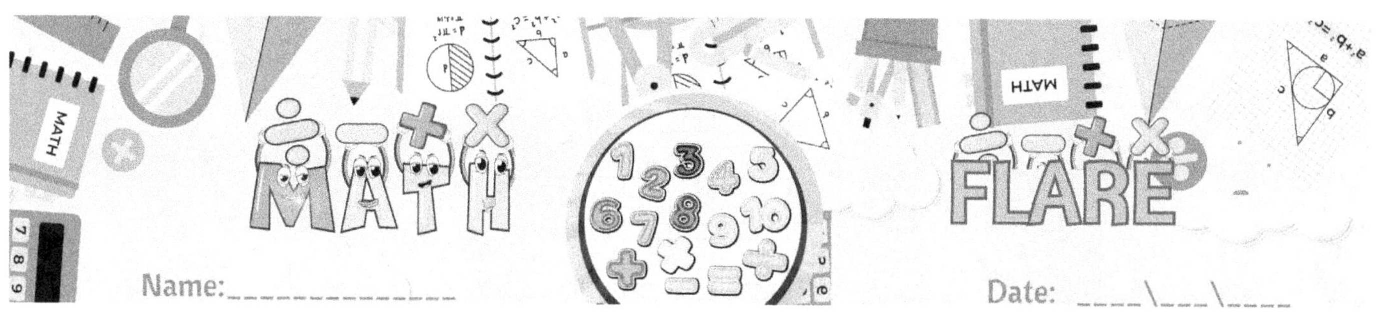

Name:_________________   Date: ________________

614. Lila had 7 dollars. She spent 3 dollars on phones. How much money does Lila have left?

615. If toothpastes costs 2 dollars and you have 1 dollars, how much more money do you need to buy it?

616. There are 6 cars in a parking lot. Emmett took 3 cars out of the lot. How many cars are still in the lot?

617. Penelope and Reagan had 3 flosses altogether. Reagan gave 2 flosses to Brandon. How many flosses do they have left?

618. A cake recipe calls for 3 cups of flour. 1 cups of flour have already been added. How many more cups of flour are needed?

619. Folders originally cost 4 dollars, but it is now on sale for 1 dollars. How much money can you save by buying it on sale?

620. Gabriella bought erasers for 7 dollars. She received 5 dollars in change. How much did erasers cost?

Fact Families

Complete each family of facts.

621.

10
7   3

☐ + ☐ = ☐
☐ + ☐ = ☐
☐ - ☐ = ☐
☐ - ☐ = ☐

622.

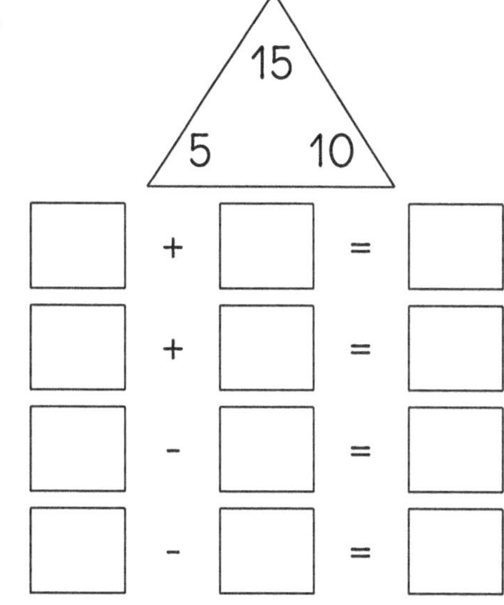

15
5   10

☐ + ☐ = ☐
☐ + ☐ = ☐
☐ - ☐ = ☐
☐ - ☐ = ☐

623.

15
10   5

☐ + ☐ = ☐
☐ + ☐ = ☐
☐ - ☐ = ☐
☐ - ☐ = ☐

624.

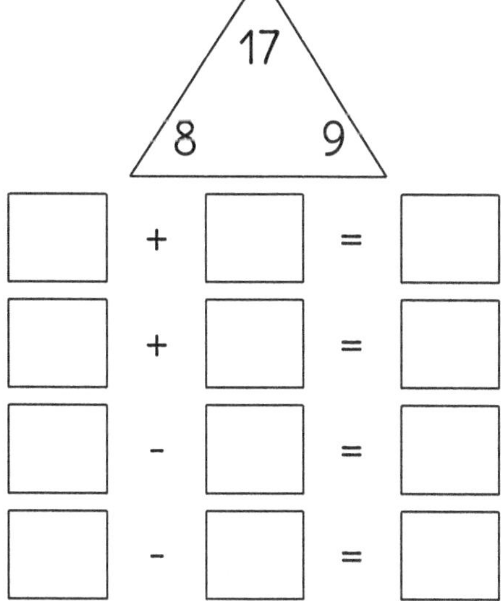

17
8   9

☐ + ☐ = ☐
☐ + ☐ = ☐
☐ - ☐ = ☐
☐ - ☐ = ☐

625.

$$\triangle \quad 15 \;/\; 9 \quad 6$$

☐ + ☐ = ☐

☐ + ☐ = ☐

☐ - ☐ = ☐

☐ - ☐ = ☐

626.

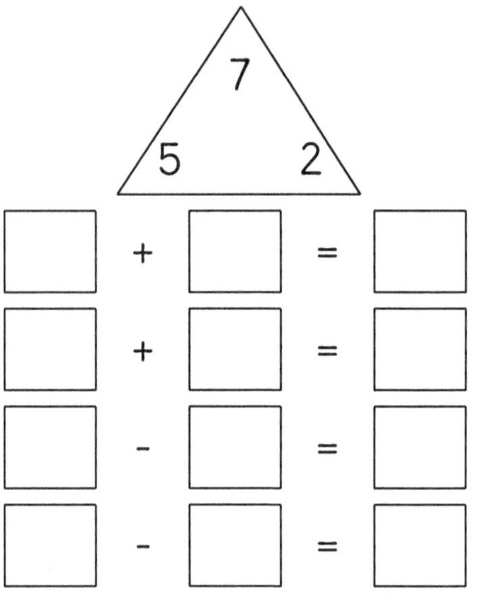

$$\triangle \quad 7 \;/\; 5 \quad 2$$

☐ + ☐ = ☐

☐ + ☐ = ☐

☐ - ☐ = ☐

☐ - ☐ = ☐

627.

$$\triangle \quad 14 \;/\; 9 \quad 5$$

☐ + ☐ = ☐

☐ + ☐ = ☐

☐ - ☐ = ☐

☐ - ☐ = ☐

628.

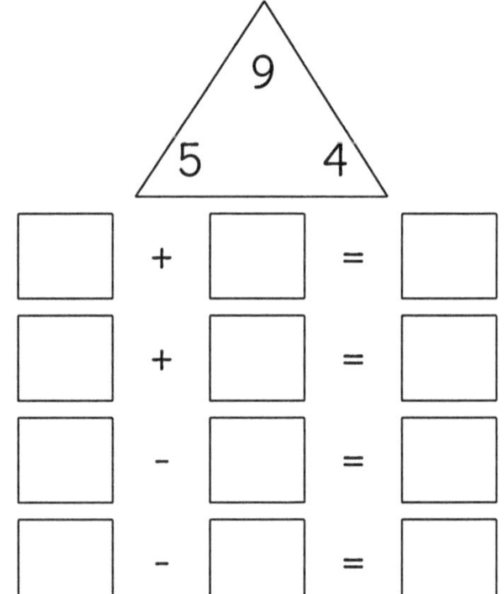

$$\triangle \quad 9 \;/\; 5 \quad 4$$

☐ + ☐ = ☐

☐ + ☐ = ☐

☐ - ☐ = ☐

☐ - ☐ = ☐

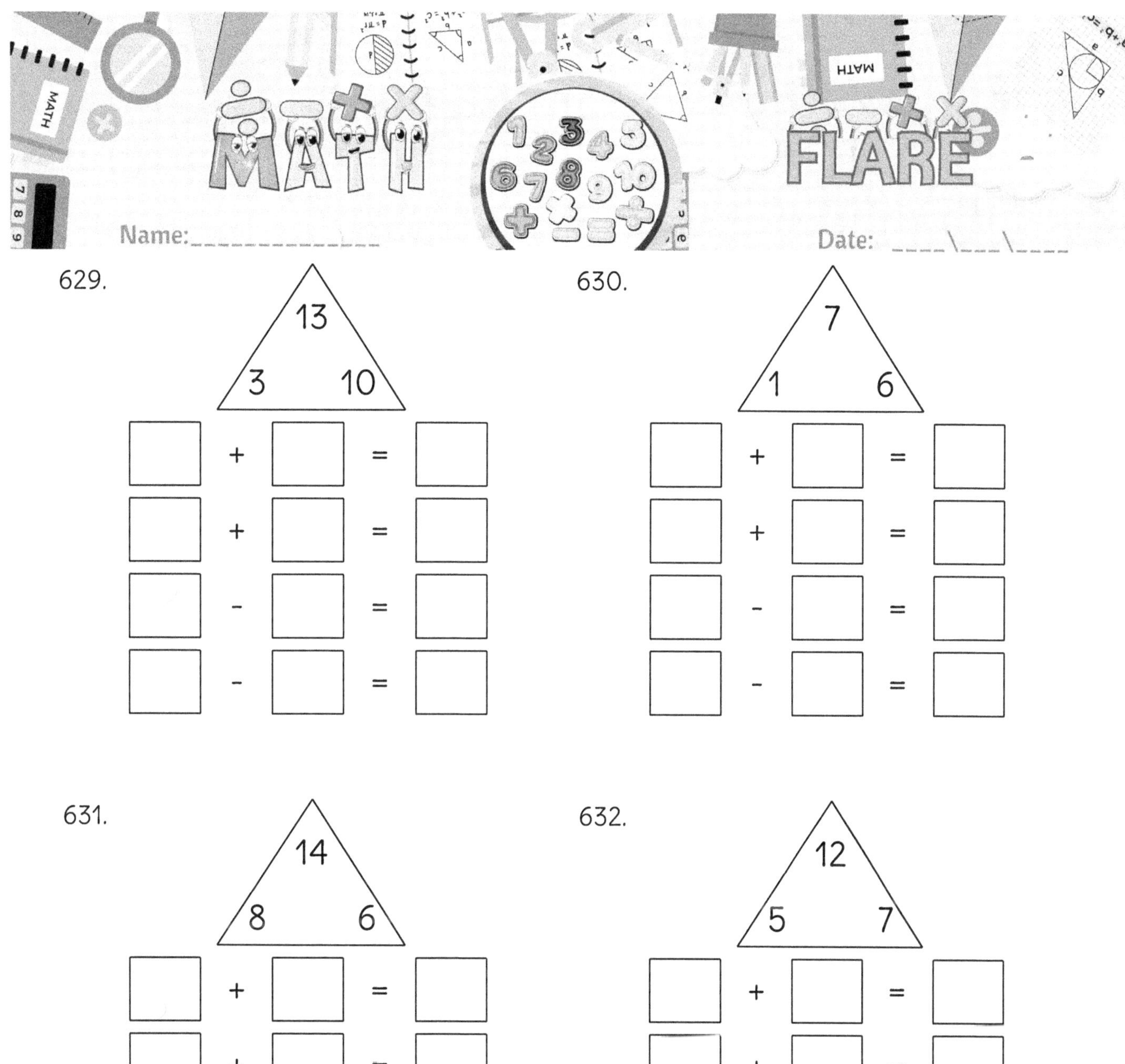

Name: _______________   Date: ____________

629.

630.

631.

632.

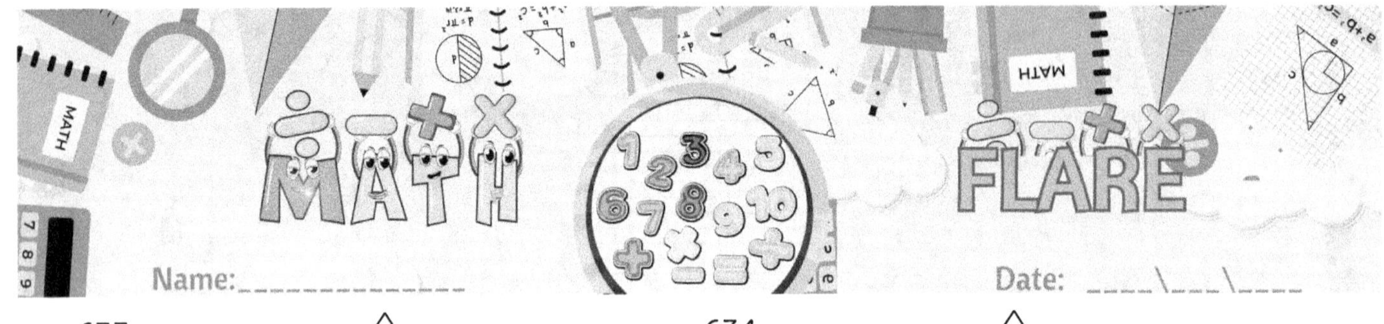

633.

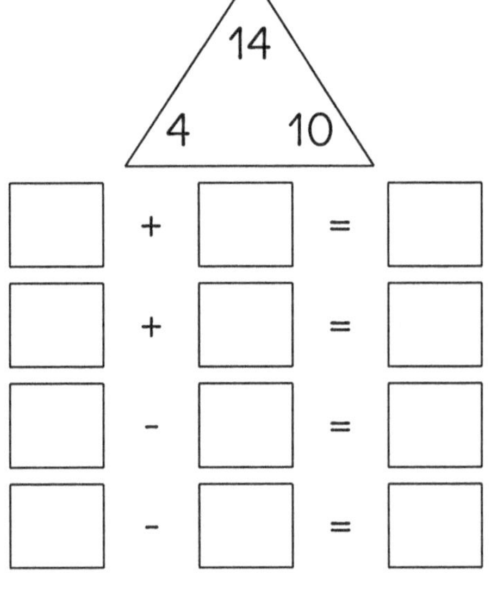

☐ + ☐ = ☐
☐ + ☐ = ☐
☐ - ☐ = ☐
☐ - ☐ = ☐

634.

☐ + ☐ = ☐
☐ + ☐ = ☐
☐ - ☐ = ☐
☐ - ☐ = ☐

635.

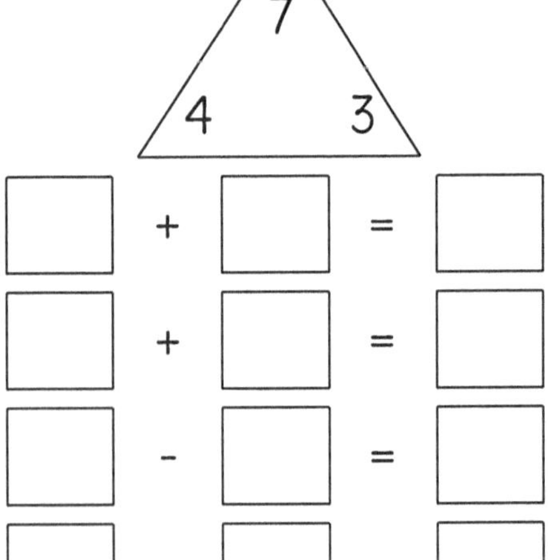

☐ + ☐ = ☐
☐ + ☐ = ☐
☐ - ☐ = ☐
☐ - ☐ = ☐

636.

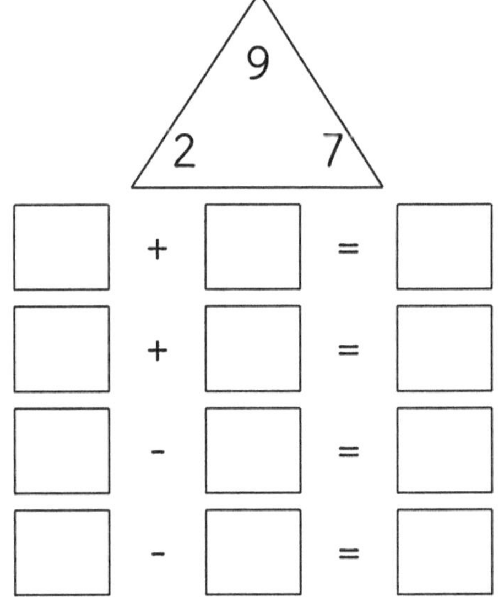

☐ + ☐ = ☐
☐ + ☐ = ☐
☐ - ☐ = ☐
☐ - ☐ = ☐

637.

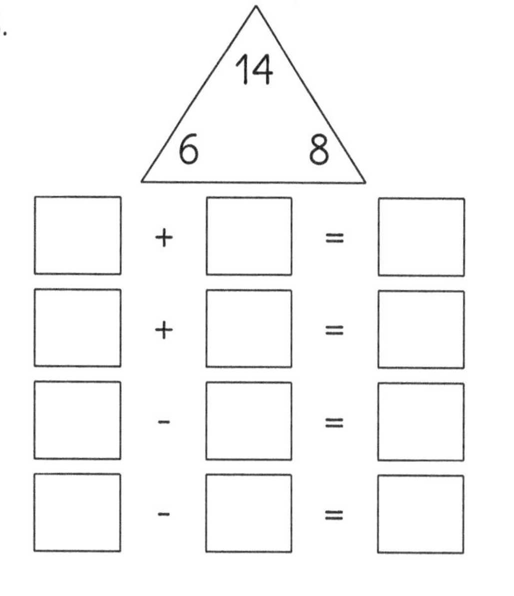

☐ + ☐ = ☐

☐ + ☐ = ☐

☐ - ☐ = ☐

☐ - ☐ = ☐

638.

14
6   8

☐ + ☐ = ☐

☐ + ☐ = ☐

☐ - ☐ = ☐

☐ - ☐ = ☐

639.

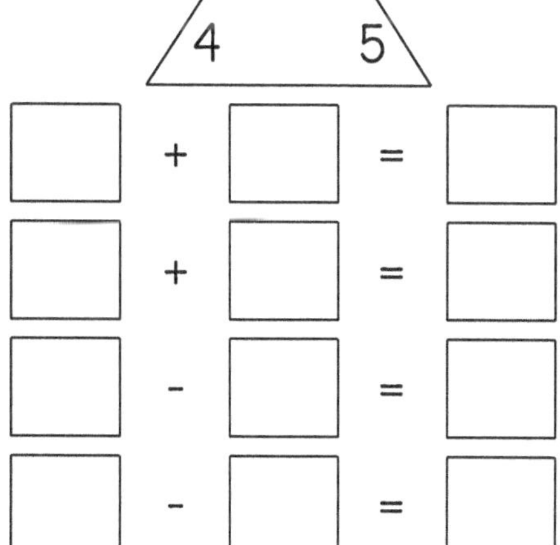

☐ + ☐ = ☐

☐ + ☐ = ☐

☐ - ☐ = ☐

☐ - ☐ = ☐

640.

9
4   5

☐ + ☐ = ☐

☐ + ☐ = ☐

☐ - ☐ = ☐

☐ - ☐ = ☐

ANSWERS

Page 1: Addition: 1 through 20

1. 24	2. 19	3. 16	4. 28	5. 27	6. 13	7. 11
8. 13	9. 23	10. 21	11. 35	12. 29	13. 29	14. 17
15. 17	16. 22	17. 32	18. 7	19. 36	20. 15	21. 8
22. 18	23. 21	24. 26	25. 7	26. 13	27. 15	28. 22
29. 28	30. 15	31. 18	32. 14	33. 20	34. 5	35. 20
36. 10	37. 25	38. 16	39. 10	40. 27	41. 19	42. 24
43. 28	44. 34	45. 10	46. 16	47. 16	48. 20	49. 23
50. 38	51. 24	52. 14	53. 30	54. 25	55. 12	56. 15
57. 11	58. 31	59. 22	60. 18	61. 21	62. 16	63. 25
64. 16	65. 4	66. 23	67. 20	68. 33	69. 17	70. 21
71. 24	72. 22	73. 21	74. 32	75. 18	76. 18	77. 11
78. 24	79. 12	80. 14	81. 14	82. 13	83. 14	84. 13
85. 23	86. 15	87. 14	88. 17	89. 15	90. 32	91. 34
92. 29	93. 26	94. 32	95. 31	96. 29	97. 23	98. 19
99. 34	100. 33	101. 5	102. 18	103. 27	104. 32	105. 14
106. 12	107. 27	108. 24	109. 28	110. 7	111. 19	112. 19
113. 37	114. 16	115. 18	116. 25	117. 23	118. 33	119. 9
120. 17						

Page 6:   Addition: 1 through 20

121. 20	122. 13	123. 34	124. 25	125. 12	126. 16	127. 21
128. 26	129. 25	130. 39	131. 13	132. 31	133. 5	134. 30
135. 13	136. 20	137. 23	138. 21	139. 20	140. 7	141. 26
142. 17	143. 31	144. 39	145. 18	146. 19	147. 33	148. 9
149. 16	150. 30	151. 23	152. 18	153. 22	154. 26	155. 37
156. 19	157. 13	158. 5	159. 6	160. 20	161. 10	162. 31
163. 26	164. 11	165. 18	166. 15	167. 21	168. 31	169. 26
170. 20	171. 22	172. 17	173. 35	174. 11	175. 13	176. 15
177. 27	178. 18	179. 17	180. 18	181. 20	182. 17	183. 22
184. 10	185. 15	186. 21	187. 26	188. 22	189. 12	190. 36
191. 27	192. 32	193. 6	194. 14	195. 13	196. 32	197. 23
198. 31	199. 30	200. 21	201. 13	202. 24	203. 30	204. 24
205. 30	206. 10	207. 29	208. 21	209. 25	210. 17	211. 16
212. 26	213. 25	214. 17	215. 20	216. 22	217. 23	218. 10
219. 30	220. 19	221. 11	222. 9	223. 23	224. 19	225. 24
226. 14	227. 20	228. 24	229. 27	230. 19	231. 21	232. 19
233. 22	234. 17	235. 24	236. 31	237. 15	238. 22	239. 20
240. 13						

Page 13:   Subtraction: 1 through 20

241. 2	242. 2	243. 4	244. 1	245. 8	246. 19	247. 3

248. 0   249. 4   250. 15   251. 0   252. 1   253. 4   254. 4

255. 8   256. 1   257. 7   258. 2   259. 1   260. 16   261. 1

262. 12   263. 0   264. 15   265. 7   266. 6   267. 4   268. 14

269. 18   270. 3   271. 1   272. 5   273. 12   274. 4   275. 7

276. 2   277. 17   278. 4   279. 9   280. 3   281. 10   282. 0

283. 9   284. 11   285. 5   286. 11   287. 2   288. 1   289. 1

290. 15   291. 5   292. 1   293. 8   294. 3   295. 2   296. 2

297. 6   298. 5   299. 0   300. 0   301. 16   302. 0   303. 16

304. 6   305. 10   306. 3   307. 3   308. 11   309. 9   310. 6

311. 7   312. 3   313. 11   314. 10   315. 13   316. 4   317. 2

318. 1   319. 3   320. 8   321. 0   322. 1   323. 1   324. 3

325. 12   326. 5   327. 12   328. 6   329. 4   330. 6   331. 4

332. 8   333. 6   334. 8   335. 14   336. 2   337. 1   338. 7

339. 5   340. 11   341. 7   342. 4   343. 4   344. 17   345. 16

346. 1   347. 5   348. 13   349. 9   350. 4   351. 15   352. 9

353. 11   354. 9   355. 6   356. 7   357. 0   358. 10   359. 14

360. 8

Page 18: Subtraction: 1 through 20

361. 3   362. 7   363. 2   364. 2   365. 7   366. 1   367. 2   368. 12

369. 0   370. 2   371. 0   372. 7   373. 5   374. 5   375. 3   376. 1

377. 0   378. 4   379. 1   380. 0   381. 10 382. 3   383. 2   384. 4

385. 6   386. 1   387. 2   388. 8   389. 1   390. 6   391. 10   392. 2

393. 13   394. 1   395. 0   396. 6   397. 2   398. 6   399. 1   400. 2

401. 5   402. 11   403. 6   404. 11   405. 5   406. 3   407. 15   408. 4

409. 12   410. 11   411. 7   412. 17   413. 10   414. 2   415. 1   416. 7

417. 13   418. 4   419. 8   420. 16   421. 5   422. 8   423. 4   424. 8

425. 4   426. 4   427. 13   428. 0   429. 3   430. 0   431. 1   432. 10

433. 4   434. 10   435. 8   436. 3   437. 1   438. 1   439. 2   440. 8

441. 11   442. 5   443. 6   444. 2   445. 4   446. 10   447. 13   448. 14

449. 3   450. 0   451. 16   452. 4   453. 1   454. 3   455. 3   456. 12

457. 16   458. 9   459. 5   460. 6   461. 14   462. 8   463. 5   464. 0

465. 15   466. 12   467. 5   468. 0   469. 7   470. 7   471. 6   472. 8

473. 18   474. 12   475. 12   476. 11   477. 8   478. 5   479. 2   480. 14

481. 4   482. 4   483. 10   484. 7   485. 3   486. 9   487. 12   488. 2

489. 0   490. 14   491. 3   492. 1   493. 17   494. 0   495. 3   496. 9

497. 3   498. 4   499. 9   500. 5   501. 7   502. 4

Page 27: Commutative Property

503. 7   504. 5   505. 2   506. 8   507. 1   508. 2   509. 2

510. 8   511. 8   512. 3   513. 10   514. 8   515. 2   516. 8

517. 2   518. 9   519. 4   520. 8   521. 9   522. 10   523. 4

524. 10   525. 5   526. 4   527. 5   528. 2   529. 3   530. 6

531. 7   532. 6   533. 3   534. 7   535. 7   536. 5   537. 9

538. 3   539. 5   540. 9   541. 9   542. 3   543. 5   544. 9

545. 4   546. 9   547. 4   548. 9   549. 3   550. 10

Page 30: Addition-Subtraction Activities

551. a.J b.F c.B d.E e.I f.C g.D h.H i.A j.G

552. a.I b.F c.B d.E e.A f.D g.J h.C i.G j.H

553. a.I b.G c.D d.B e.E f.J g.A h.C i.F j.H

554. a.D b.B c.E d.G e.C f.I g.A h.J i.H j.F

555. a.B b.G c.A d.D e.I f.F g.H h.E i.J j.C

556. a.I b.B c.F d.J e.G f.D g.A h.E i.H j.C

557. a.J b.G c.B d.C e.H f.A g.I h.F i.E j.D

558. a.C b.B c.G d.H e.E f.J g.F h.I i.D j.A

559. a.G b.E c.A d.C e.F f.B g.I h.D i.J j.H

560. a.D b.I c.H d.B e.J f.C g.A h.G i.F j.E

Page 40: Addition Word Problems

561. 13   562. 12   563. 11   564. 17   565. 12   566. 17   567. 15   568. 15

569. 11   570. 8   571. 10   572. 10   573. 11   574. 12   575. 12   576. 7

577. 8   578. 14   579. 10   580. 11   581. 16   582. 13   583. 11   584. 8

585. 19   586. 8   587. 14   588. 7   589. 10   590. 12

Page 48: Subtraction Word Problems

591. 9   592. 0   593. 0   594. 0   595. 1   596. 0   597. 2   598. 0

599. 0   600. 7   601. 5   602. 8   603. 2   604. 0   605. 2   606. 0

607. 0   608. 0   609. 5   610. 0   611. 6   612. 2   613. 0   614. 4

615. 1   616. 3   617. 1   618. 2   619. 3   620. 2

Page 56:   Fact Families

621.

622.
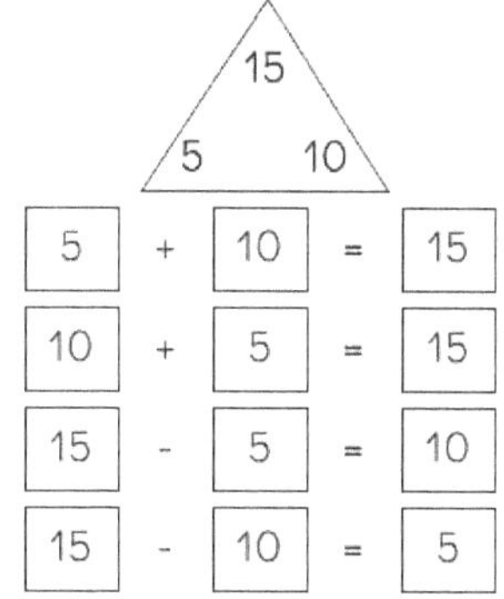

623.
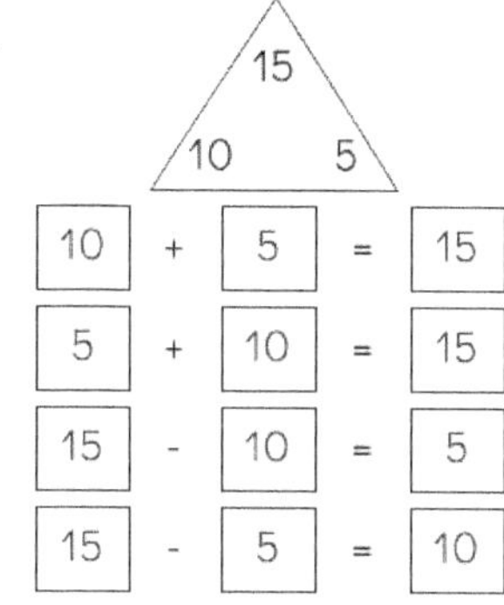

624.
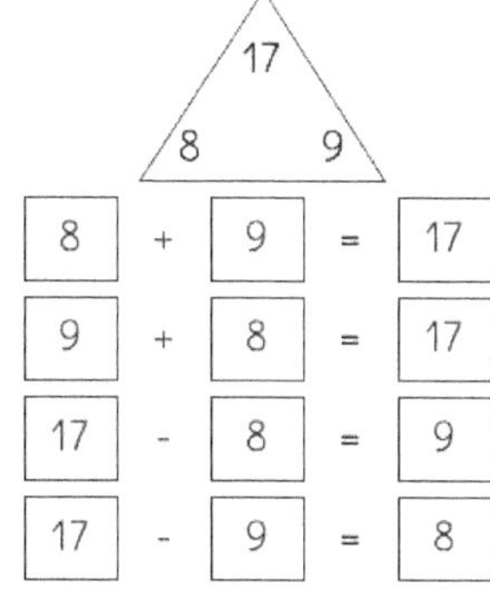

625.
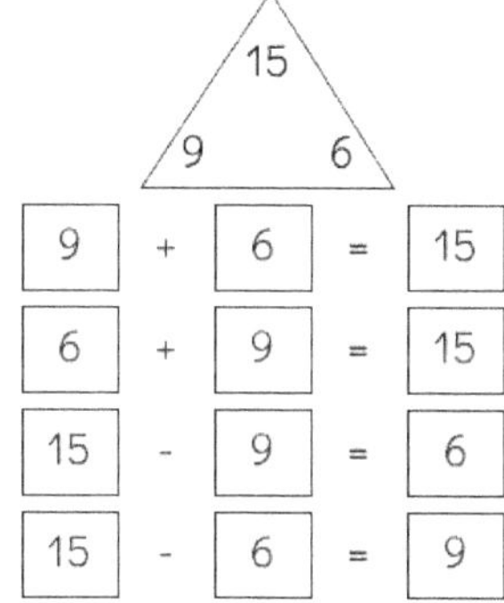

626.
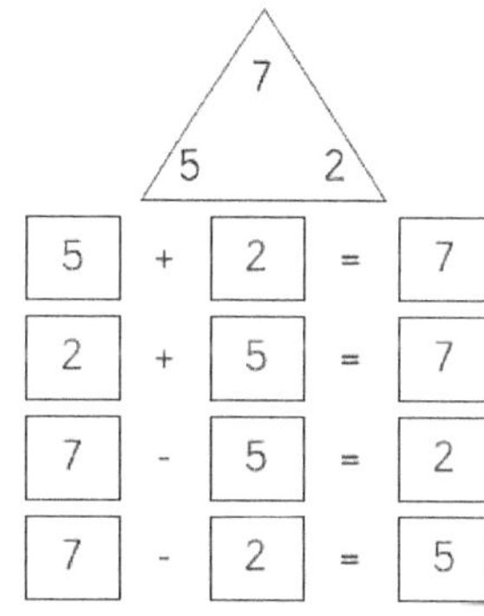

627.
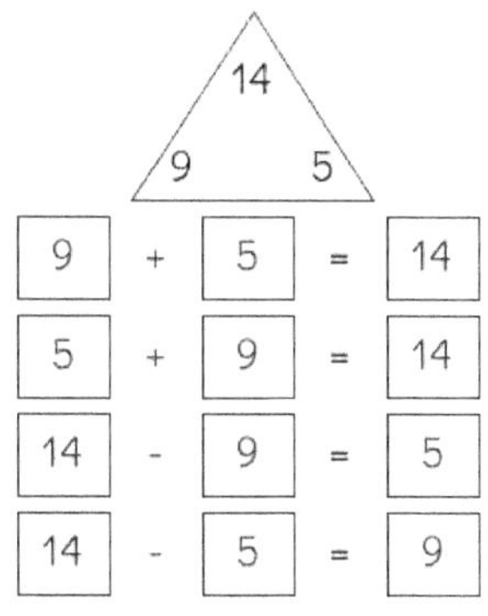

628.
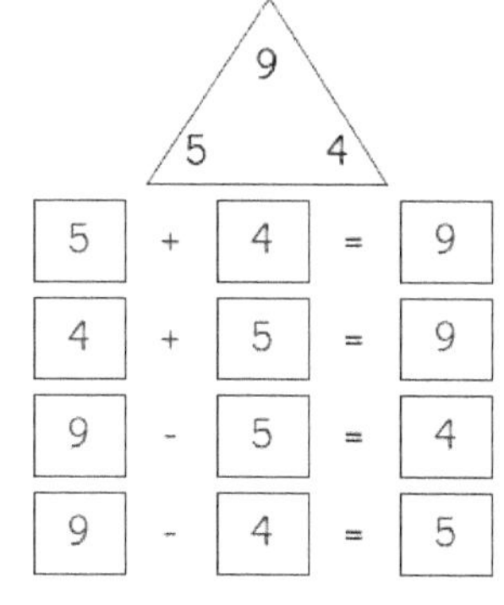

629.
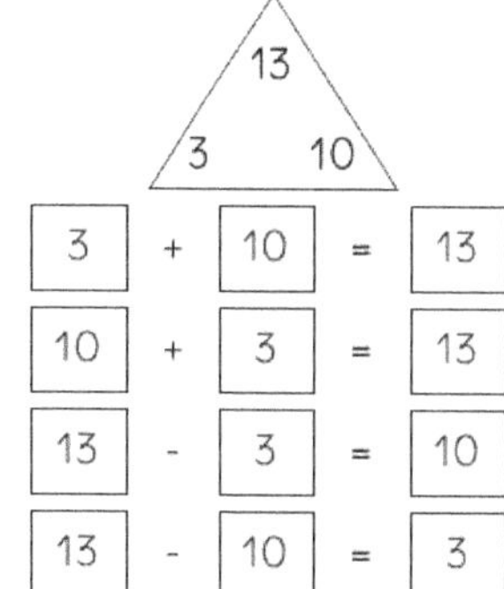

630.

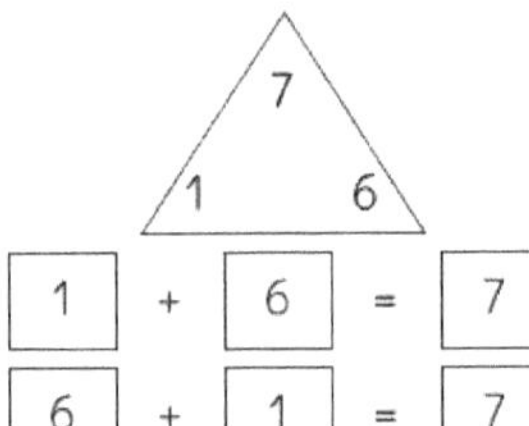

1	+	6	=	7
6	+	1	=	7
7	-	1	=	6
7	-	6	=	1

631.

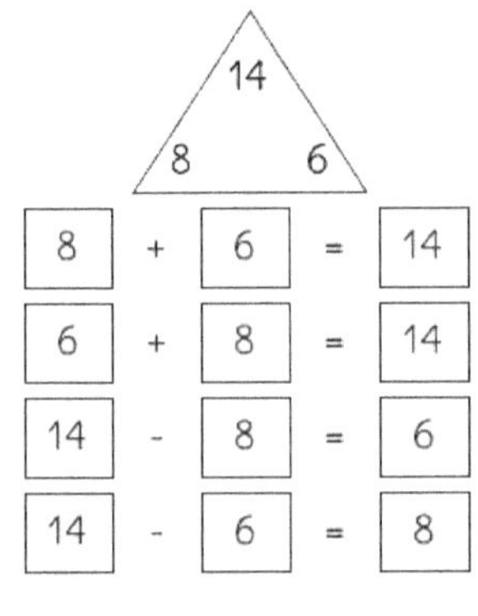

8	+	6	=	14
6	+	8	=	14
14	-	8	=	6
14	-	6	=	8

632.

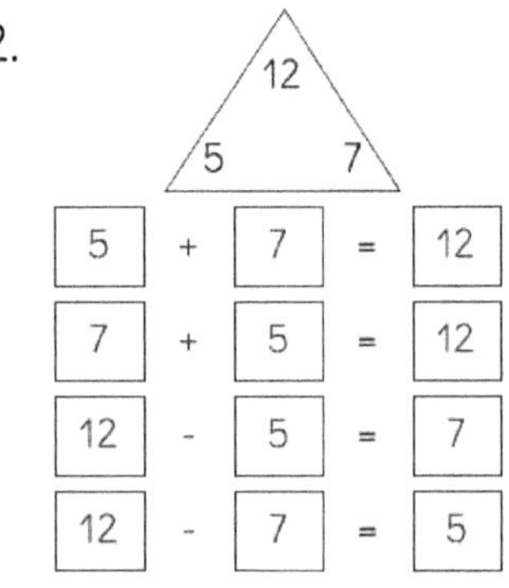

5	+	7	=	12
7	+	5	=	12
12	-	5	=	7
12	-	7	=	5

633.

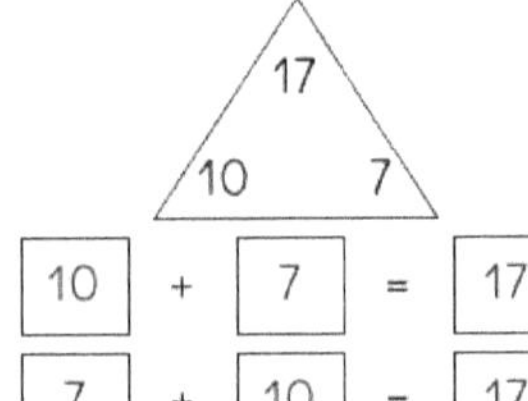

10	+	7	=	17
7	+	10	=	17
17	-	10	=	7
17	-	7	=	10

634.

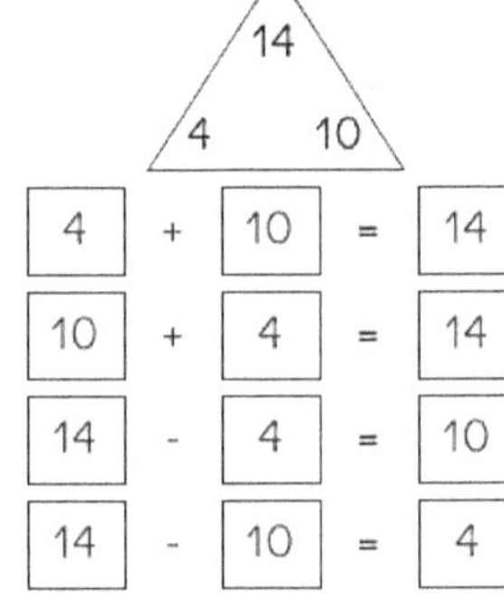

4	+	10	=	14
10	+	4	=	14
14	-	4	=	10
14	-	10	=	4

635.

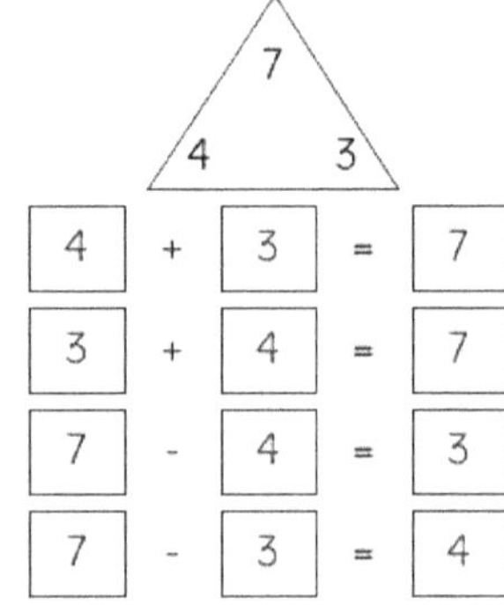

4	+	3	=	7
3	+	4	=	7
7	-	4	=	3
7	-	3	=	4

636.

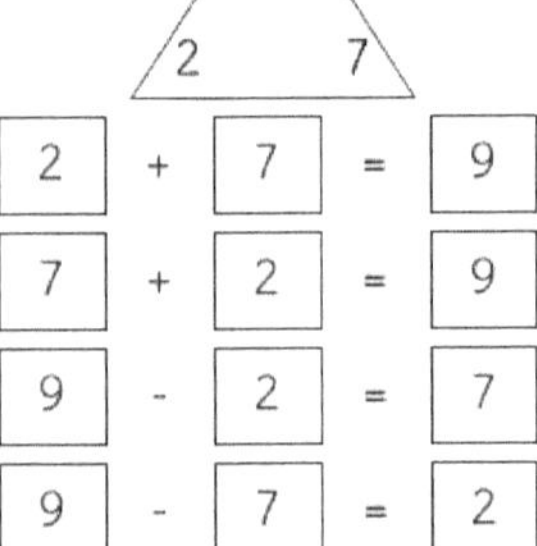

2	+	7	=	9
7	+	2	=	9
9	-	2	=	7
9	-	7	=	2

637.

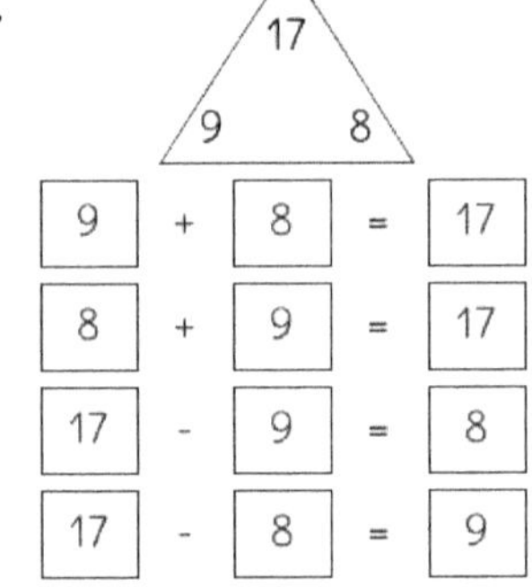

9	+	8	=	17
8	+	9	=	17
17	-	9	=	8
17	-	8	=	9

638.

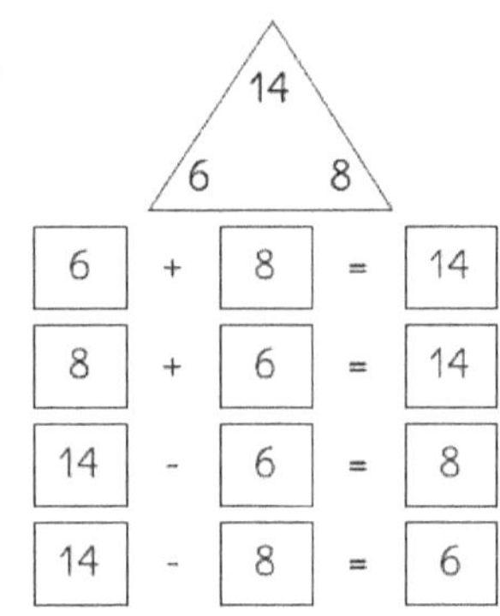

6	+	8	=	14
8	+	6	=	14
14	-	6	=	8
14	-	8	=	6

639.

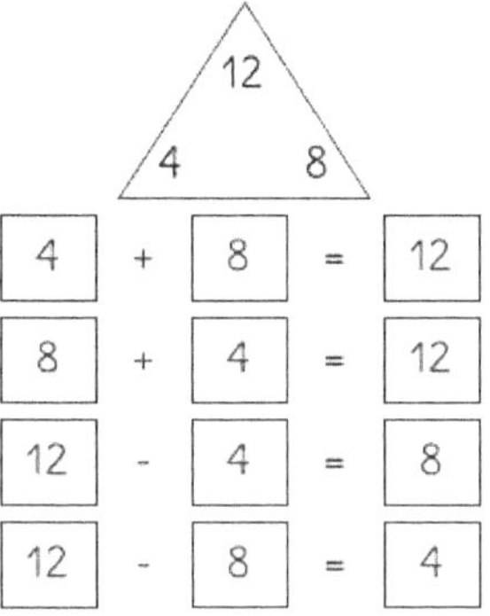

4	+	8	=	12
8	+	4	=	12
12	-	4	=	8
12	-	8	=	4

640.

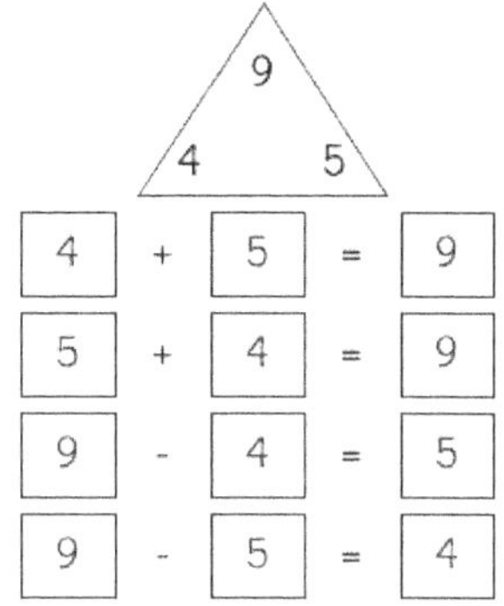

4	+	5	=	9
5	+	4	=	9
9	-	4	=	5
9	-	5	=	4